★★★ KID ★★★ ACTIVISTS

TRUE TALES OF CHILDHOOD FROM

CHAMPIONS OF CHANGE

STORIES BY *ROBIN STEVENSON*   ILLUSTRATIONS BY *ALLISON STEINFELD*

ARTIN LUTHER KING JR.   HARVEY MILK   MALALA YOUSAFZAI   ALEXANDER HAMILTON

 * * * # KID ACTIVISTS * * *

TRUE TALES OF CHILDHOOD FROM

* **CHAMPIONS OF CHANGE** *

STORIES BY *ROBIN STEVENSON*   ILLUSTRATIONS BY *ALLISON STEINFELD*

HELEN KELLER   **NELSON MANDELA**   **EMMA WATSON**   **FREDERICK DOUGLASS**

Copyright © 2019 by Quirk Productions, Inc.

Library of Congress Cataloging in Publication Number: 2019930322

ISBN: 978-1-68369-141-9

Printed in the United States of America
Typeset in Bulmer MT, Bell MT, Linowrite, and Bulldog

Designed by Andie Reid
Illustrations by Allison Steinfeld
Production management by John J. McGurk

Quirk Books
215 Church Street
Philadelphia, PA 19106
quirkbooks.com

10 9 8 7 6 5 4

*To all the courageous
and passionate kids around
the world who are standing up
for justice and equality.*

Table of Contents

PART 3

UNUSUAL CHILDHOODS, POWERFUL VOICES

PART 4

CHILD ACTIVISTS

Introduction

Have you ever noticed something that didn't seem fair? Do you sometimes wish that you could make the world a better place for everyone? If so, then maybe you will become an activist!

Activists are people who try to make changes in society. They work to persuade governments to end laws that are unjust and to make new laws that treat people more fairly and help protect the planet we live on. They try to make people aware of issues they care about. Some activists write and speak about problems they want to fix. Others take part in protests and demonstrations, organize boycotts, or start petitions. There are lots of ways to make a difference.

Throughout history, people have participated in social justice movements. People fought to abolish slavery. They fought for women's right to vote. They fought to end racial segregation, and they fought for civil rights and equality for African Americans. They fought for better protection for workers, access to education for people with disabilities, marriage equality, and much more. Many of the basic human rights people now have exist because of the hard work and sacrifices of activists like the ones you are about to meet.

All of the activists in this book decided to take action against injustice. You've probably heard about some of them, but others may be new to you. Some of them became activists when they were young. Ruby Bridges was only six years old when she faced down angry crowds as the first black student at an all-white school.

In Pakistan, Iqbal Masih fought against child labor after he was forced to start working in a carpet factory at the age of four.

Malala Yousafzai spoke out when the Taliban attacked girls' schools in her country and forced her father's school to close.

Others became activists as adults because of the injustices they experienced as children. Frederick Douglass was born into slavery but even as a child, he was determined to be free. And when he was free, he worked to end slavery in the United States.

The people in this book changed the world—but they were all once kids, just like you. Civil rights leader Martin Luther King Jr. had a paper route and played practical jokes on his piano teacher. And young Helen Keller once stole and ate an entire cake!

Their childhoods may be different, but all these activists have one thing in common: they cared about equality and freedom, and they worked hard to make the world a better place. May their stories inspire you to stand up for what you believe in, too!

ONE

LEADING
THE
WAY

FREEDOM, JUSTICE,

** AND **

HUMAN RIGHTS.

THESE

KID ACTIVISTS

GREW UP TO BECOME

VISIONARY LEADERS

who helped

PAVE THE ROAD TOWARD

EQUALITY.

Frederick Douglass

A Determination to Be Free

Frederick Douglass spent his life fighting to end the enslavement of black Americans. He believed in equality for all people, and he later supported the right for women to vote. But before he could fight to change the world around him, he first had to escape from bondage and be free.

Frederick Augustus Washington Bailey was born around 1818. At that time, more than one million African people were enslaved in America, and many white families owned slaves, whom they considered to be their property. Frederick was born into slavery because his mother was enslaved. He never knew his exact birth date. As a child, it made him unhappy that the white children knew their ages, but he was not even allowed to ask about his.

As a boy, Frederick lived with his cousins, his younger sisters, and his grandparents. They shared a small cabin on a farm that was part of a huge plantation in Maryland.

Frederick had been separated from his mother when he was a baby. Her name was Harriet Bailey, and she was enslaved on another farm twelve miles away. A few times, after working in the fields all day, she walked twelve miles through the night to see her son. She'd lie down with him, and once he was asleep, she walked home. If she wasn't back in the field by sunrise, she would be punished by being whipped. Frederick was still young when his mother died, and he never had the chance to know her well. He later wrote, "I do not recollect of ever seeing my mother by the light of day."

Still, these first few years of Frederick's childhood were happier than those that followed. He loved his grandmother very much. Although she was also enslaved, she was considered too old for labor and instead took care of Frederick and the other children. She did her best to protect Frederick from the full truth about slavery, but sometimes he heard talk of an "old master," who only allowed children to live with their grandmother for a short time before they would be taken away to live with him.

Frederick spent his time exploring the woods and creek, or playing "gleesome sports" with other children, but he had a growing sense of dread. He later wrote: "Grandmammy was, indeed, at that time, all the world to me; and the thought of being separated from her, in any considerable time, was more than an unwelcome intruder. It was intolerable."

When he was six years old, that dreaded day came: Frederick was sent to live with the "old master," a man known as Captain Anthony. It was a long journey, which he and his grandmother walked together. When they arrived, Frederick's grandmother told him to go play. Then she quietly left. Devastated, Frederick cried himself to sleep that night.

The next day, Frederick was forced to start working. He had to keep the yard clean, bring the cows in at night, and run errands. Although he was only six, no one took care of him. He had no shoes, jacket, or pants; he and the other enslaved children were given only two shirts a year. If those wore out, they had nothing to wear.

Frederick and the other children were fed cooked corn meal, which was called mush. It was poured into a trough on the ground, and they had to eat with their hands or scoop the food with shells or broken shingles. There was never enough, and Frederick often went hungry. And in the winter, he was freezing! He had no bed, so he stole a bag used for carrying corn and crawled inside, sleeping on the cold damp floor.

When he was eight years old, Frederick's life changed again. His owner died, and he was given to new owners: Thomas and Lucretia Auld. They sent him to live in Baltimore, with Thomas's brother Hugh Auld and his family. In his new home, Frederick had a room in a loft above the kitchen. Mrs. Auld made him a bed of a mattress stuffed with straw. He had a woolen blanket, clothes, and better food to eat. Most important, Mrs.

Auld taught Frederick the alphabet and showed him how to read simple words. When her husband found out, he was furious. If she taught Frederick to read, he said, "it would forever unfit him to be a slave. He would at once become unmanageable and of no value to his master."

Those words changed the course of Frederick's life. "From that moment," he later wrote, "I understood the pathway from slavery to freedom." If reading would make him unfit for slavery, then he would learn to read!

Frederick seized every opportunity to look at newspapers and books. The more he read, the more he understood about slavery—and the more he hated those who kept him enslaved. He dreamed of being free, but it seemed impossible. "Freedom," he wrote, "was ever present to torment me with a sense of my wretched condition."

When Frederick was fifteen, his life took another turn for the worse: he was sent back to live with his owner. Thomas Auld and his wife "were well matched," Frederick wrote, "being equally mean and cruel." Frederick—who was tall and strong and good with words—argued with Thomas Auld. He was whipped many times, and finally he was rented out to work for a man named Edward Covey, who had a reputation for violence and brutality. Frederick was forced to till fields from sunup until sundown, and often long into the night. He had to work with draft horses and teams of oxen, and the big animals scared him.

But worst of all was the vicious bullying from Edward Covey. Exhausted and in constant pain, Frederick could see no way out.

One day, he decided to stand up to Covey. They fought each other for two hours before Covey gave up. After that, Covey seemed afraid of Frederick; he never tried to whip him again. The fight, Frederick said, was a turning point: "It rekindled the few expiring embers of freedom. . . . It recalled the departed self-confidence and inspired me again with a determination to be free."

When Frederick was about sixteen, he was sent to work on other farms. He became friends with two enslaved young men, Henry and John Harris. Secretly, he began teaching them to read. Other slaves wanted to learn, too, so Frederick began holding classes on Sundays at the home of a free black man. At one time, he had more than forty students.

Frederick loved teaching. He later wrote, "The work of instructing my dear fellow slaves was the sweetest engagement with which I was ever blessed."

Frederick's desire for freedom was growing stronger every day. Trying to escape was dangerous, and those who were caught were severely punished. But Frederick and his friends decided to take the chance. They made a plan: they would steal a canoe, paddle it up the Chesapeake Bay, and then walk, following the North Star, until they reached the Maryland border.

Unfortunately, word of their plan got out. They were dragged off to jail, and Frederick was separated from his friends. He was alone and in despair. "I expected to have been safe in a land of freedom," he wrote, "but now

I was covered with gloom. . . . I thought the possibility of freedom was gone."

But Frederick did not give up. After being released from prison, he was hired out to work in a shipyard, where he met many black sailors who were free. He also met a free black woman, Anna Murray, and fell in love with her.

When Frederick was around twenty years old, he borrowed protection papers from a sailor friend. These papers certified that the bearer was a free man—a sailor, not a slave. This was dangerous for both men: Frederick later described it as an act of supreme trust for a free man to risk his liberty to help another become free. Since the papers said Frederick was a sailor, Anna altered his clothes to make him look the part. She sold a feather bed to pay for his journey to freedom, and Frederick caught a train heading north.

When the train conductor asked to see the documents that all free black people had to carry, Frederick said, "I never carry my free papers to sea with me." He handed over his seaman's papers instead. The conductor glanced at them quickly and handed them back. It was fortunate that he didn't look too carefully: the papers described a man who looked nothing like him.

Next, Frederick caught a ferry across the Susquehanna River to Pennsylvania, where he had another close call. A man he knew saw him and expressed surprise to see him dressed as a sailor. Frederick dodged the man's questions and moved to another part of the boat.

Finally, he was across the river, and then he boarded one last train: to New York, a free state in the north.

Anna Murray traveled north to join him, and the couple married and moved to Massachusetts. Worried that slave catchers might still be looking for him, Frederick decided to change his last name from Bailey to Douglass.

Now that he was free, Frederick Douglass wanted to free others. He met many abolitionists—people who were working to end slavery. In 1841, he gave his first speech against slavery at an abolitionist meeting. He spoke powerfully about his own experience, and he was asked to speak at many more meetings.

Four years later, he wrote a book about his life. Thousands of people read it, and his words convinced many of them that slavery was morally wrong. Soon after, he started an antislavery newspaper called the *North Star.*

By the time the North and South clashed in the Civil War, the conflict that finally brought an end to slavery in the United States, Frederick Douglas was one of the most famous black men in the country. His difficult journey from enslaved man to free abolitionist had helped change the course of history.

Harriet Tubman was born in Maryland just a couple years after Frederick Douglass, and she, too, was enslaved. In her late twenties, Harriet managed to escape using the network known as the Underground Railroad—a loosely organized group of people, free and enslaved, black and white—who helped slaves travel north to free states or to Canada. A year after her escape, Harriet risked returning to Maryland and helped other family members escape. Over the next decade, she assisted more than three hundred slaves to freedom.

But Harriet wanted all enslaved African Americans to be freed. So when the Civil War began, she supported the Union Army—first as a nurse and cook and, later, as a spy. The intelligence she gathered led to a successful raid that freed more than seven hundred slaves, many of whom joined the Union Army to fight against the South.

Susan B. Anthony

> Failure Is
> Impossible

I n 1872, Susan B. Anthony was arrested and fined one hundred dollars for voting in an American presidential election. Why? Because at that time women were not allowed to vote. More than forty years later, thanks to Susan and other suffragists, the Nineteenth Amendment to the U.S. Constitution was passed. The new amendment meant that citizens could no longer be denied the right to vote because they were women.

Susan was born in 1820 in a farmhouse in Adams, Massachusetts. She was the second of seven children: five girls and two boys. Susan's father was deeply religious; he banned toys, games, and music from the house because he didn't want his children to be distracted from their religious education. He was a Quaker who stood up for what he believed in. As a pacifist, he refused to pay taxes to a government that engaged in war. He also believed that men and women were equal in the eyes of God.

When Susan was six years old, her family moved to eastern New York. Her father managed a cotton mill there and hired many young women to work for him. These "mill girls," as they were known, boarded at the

Anthonys' home. Sometimes as many as eleven girls lived in the house at one time. Not all the workers shared the Anthonys' religion, and they wanted to dance. Susan's father did not approve of dancing, but he also didn't want them to go to a tavern. So he allowed them to dance in the attic of the mill after hours.

This decision caused a conflict with other local Quakers, and eventually he was asked to leave his religious community. But his faith and beliefs continued to influence his life and, in turn, his daughter's.

Susan's mother also played an important role in shaping Susan's life and values. From an early age, Susan and her sisters were expected to work hard. With such a big family, and all the mill girls to look after, they had an endless amount of chores: cleaning, sewing, fetching water, cooking, and cleaning up.

But there were good times, too. On their way to school, Susan and her siblings walked past the home of their Grandmother Read, their mother's mother. They always left home early so they had time to stop there for a drink of "coffee," which their grandmother made by browning crusts of bread, pouring hot water over them, and sweetening the liquid with maple sugar. After school they would visit again to eat leftovers of pork or beef, potatoes, cabbage, turnips, beets, and carrots.

Their other grandmother—Grandmother Anthony—also had a house full of treats. In a little closet under the stairs was a tub of maple sugar, and the

Anthony children would gather around to feast on it. Grandmother Anthony would send them home with apples, donuts, and cakes, but their favorite snack was her "hasty pudding." It was made by cooking cornmeal for hours, then scooping it onto a platter and filling it with butter and maple syrup, like a delicious volcano.

When Susan was around twelve years old, one of the factory girls became sick. Susan and her younger sister Hannah begged their father to take her place. They were allowed to draw straws to decide who would get the job, and Susan won. She worked for two weeks and received a wage of three dollars, which she had to share with Hannah. With her earnings, Susan bought a set of blue coffee cups and saucers and gave them to her mother.

Susan was an intelligent child; she learned to read when she was only three years old. She had a remarkable memory and was curious about everything. But her education wasn't always smooth sailing. In one school, her teacher refused to teach her long division. Her father was not pleased. He wanted his children to have a better education, so he hired private teachers to instruct them at home. The young women who worked in his mills attended classes, too.

When Susan was fifteen, her father encouraged her to get a job. At first, she taught younger children in the Anthonys' home school; later, she worked as a teacher in a local school. She was paid $1.50 a week—a quarter of the amount that the school's male teachers earned.

Although her father supported her desire to work, he was still influenced by the views of the time. When the foreman at the mill left, Susan suggested that one of the women replace him, but her father said that he would never put a woman in charge of his business.

Two years later, Susan and her older sister were sent to study at Deborah Moulson's Female Seminary, an expensive boarding school for Quaker girls. Susan was deeply attatched to her home and family, and she soon became miserably homesick.

To make matters worse, Miss Moulson was strict and unkind. She scolded Susan, saying, "Thy sister Guelma does the best she is capable of, but thou dost not." Susan even got in trouble for not dotting her i's properly!

The constant criticism was hard on her. In her diary, she wrote that she was a "vile sinner . . . I do consider myself such a bad creature that I cannot see any who seems worse." Later in life, Susan said the thought of that school still made her feel "cold and sick at heart."

Fortunately, she didn't stay long at the boarding school. At the end of her first term, her father arrived to take Susan and her sister Guelma home. He could no longer afford to pay for his daughters' education. The United States was going through a depression, and he was bankrupt.

Susan's family lost everything, and their possessions were auctioned off to pay their debts. Their furniture, the food on their shelves, her parents' eyeglasses, and even Susan's underwear were listed for sale.

The family moved to a nearby town in New York called Hardscrabble, and Susan began working as a teacher. Like many Quakers, she became involved in the antislavery movement. In fact, her family's home served as a meeting place for abolitionists, including Frederick Douglass, with whom she became friends.

Susan also supported the temperance movement, believing that alcohol was the cause of many social problems. But when she stood up to speak at a temperance convention, the chairman silenced her. "The sisters were not invited . . . to speak, but to listen and learn," he told her. Susan was furious. She decided to launch her own organization, and she asked her new friend Elizabeth Cady Stanton to be its president.

Together, Susan and Elizabeth started the American Equal Rights Association, campaigning for equality and the right to vote for women and African Americans. They published a women's rights newspaper called *The Revolution*, whose motto was: "Men, their rights and nothing more; women, their rights and nothing less!"

When she was still young, Susan had decided she would never marry. This choice was rare in those days: women were expected to be dependent on their husbands. She became famous for her support of the idea that women had a right to be single and independent.

Although Susan's fierce commitment to fighting for equality made her a rebel in her time, her actions were in keeping with the values she was raised with. Her parents supported her desire to be independent, believing that every human being should do everything possible to be useful to the world. Susan's brothers and sisters were also active in the fight against slavery and the fight for women's rights and suffrage.

In 1920, fourteen years after Susan B. Anthony's death, eight million American women voted—legally—in the presidential election. Susan did not live to see that day, but during her life she fully believed it would happen. In her final suffrage speech, she said: "Failure is impossible."

As for her $100 fine? "I shall never pay a dollar of your unjust penalty," she told the judge. And she never did.

For fifty years, Susan B. Anthony worked in partnership with her close friend Elizabeth Cady Stanton. Elizabeth was a writer, and she crafted many of the powerful speeches that were then given by Susan. When Elizabeth died, Susan wrote that her friend had "forged the thunderbolts" that she had fired. The two women didn't always agree, but even when their views differed, their friendship endured. "No power in heaven, hell or earth can separate us, for our hearts are eternally wedded together," Elizabeth wrote.

Harvey Milk

Coming Out for Equality

Harvey Milk was a gay rights activist and one of the first openly gay politicians to be elected to office in the United States. He won a seat on the San Francisco Board of Supervisors in 1977, but was assassinated only a year later. He grew up in an era when gay people had no rights at all, and his fight for equality made him a hero to many in the LGBTQ+ community.

Harvey was born in 1930, between the two world wars. His father, Bill, was in the Navy during World War I, and his mother, Minerva, signed up for the women's naval reserves. After the war, they both settled in New York, where they married and had two sons: Harvey and his older brother Bob.

When he was eight and nine years old, Harvey would spend his small weekly allowance on tickets to movie matinees on Saturday afternoons. He and Bob would go to watch the Lone Ranger, Hopalong Cassidy, or the Three Stooges—but it wasn't the movies that Harvey looked forward to all week. Before the film began, the theater manager held a raffle, and whoever had the winning ticket went up on stage to collect their prize—a Buck Rogers toy pistol, perhaps, or a

Hopalong Cassidy wristwatch. For Harvey, the real prize was the chance to run onto the stage and bow to the audience. He loved to be in the spotlight.

Harvey's family was Jewish, and his grandfather Morris had helped found the Sons of Israel synagogue. Harvey's dad and his uncles all worked for Morris and were members of that synagogue. Harvey loved his grandfather and wanted to please him, so he never spoke critically of religion. Later in life, though, he said that by age twelve he had decided that religion was hypocritical. Secretly, he started to reject his family's religious beliefs, but he was always proud to be Jewish.

Harvey's mother was committed to the concept of *tikkun olam*—a Hebrew phrase meaning a sense of responsibility to repair what is wrong in the world. Her ideas about social justice had a significant influence on Harvey. He was a stubborn boy, and all kinds of injustices made him angry. When he was young, that anger was usually directed at his father, who never seemed to approve of him. As he grew older, and became aware of larger injustices, he shared his mother's commitment to taking action to heal the world.

When Harvey was eleven years old, he discovered something that brought him much joy: opera. The performances of the Metropolitan Opera were broadcast on the radio, so Harvey began to spend Saturday afternoons in an armchair in his living room, listening to them. The operas were sung in French, German, or Italian, so he didn't understand the words, but he loved the emotion and the drama. Sometimes he pretended that he was wearing a tuxedo and conducting the orchestra. When he was fourteen, his mom started giving him money to take the train into New York City to see live performances.

In high school, Harvey was known by the nickname Glimpy Milch. The name Glimpy came from Glimpy McClusky, a character in the East Side Kids movies of the 1940s. Milch was the last name of his grandfather, who had immigrated to the United States from Lithuania. Milk was the English translation of Milch.

In his teens, Harvey was realizing that he was attracted to other boys. But this was long before the gay rights movement began in America. In fact, this was long before the word "gay" was even in common use. In the 1940s, same-sex relationships were a crime. Gay men were referred to as homosexuals, and Harvey knew what people thought about homosexuals; even his own mother had warned him to stay away from them. Suggesting that someone might be a homosexual was one of the worst things you could say about them. Harvey knew that this part of himself was something he had to keep secret.

So, he worked hard to fit in. He had a sense of humor that made everyone laugh. He dated girls. He was on the football team and joined track, wrestling, and basketball. Harvey hung out with the other jocks, but he didn't have any close friends, maybe because he was having to hide something important about himself. Decades later, one of his high school classmates recalled, "When we were young people, we didn't know there was such a thing as gayness. . . . If Harvey knew this, he had to face it all by himself."

Harvey wasn't a straight-A student, but he was hard-working. He wanted to get out of his hometown and start college early, so he pushed through high school faster than most students. After he graduated, no one heard from him again. "It was like he dropped off the face of the earth," one of his friends said.

As an adult, Harvey rarely talked about his childhood. One of the few stories he did share was how, in his early teens, his parents talked to him about what happened in Warsaw, Poland, during World War II. The Jewish people there were surrounded by Nazi troops, but they fought bravely. They didn't fight because they thought they could win—they were massively outnumbered. They fought, his parents told him, because evil should always be fought, even when there is no hope left.

This message stayed with Harvey, and after he became an activist, he often spoke about the importance of taking a stand against evil.

By the time Harvey graduated from high school, the Second World War had ended and the world had learned about the Holocaust. For Jewish people in America, the news was devastating: millions of Jewish people had been murdered. Many gay men were also rounded up and killed: as Jewish people were forced to wear yellow stars, gay men were forced to wear pink triangles.

As a Jewish man and as a gay man, Harvey saw himself as an outsider—as someone who had to fight to be accepted. When people said terrible things about gay people, or tried to pass laws discriminating against them, he knew how dangerous this was. As a politician, he often pointed out that similar things had been said and done to the Jewish people in Germany. "I cannot remain silent anymore," he said in one speech. "There was silence in Germany because no one got up early enough to say what Hitler really was. If only someone did, maybe the Holocaust would never have happened."

Harvey didn't become involved in gay rights activism until much later in life, but as he got older, he began to feel that the act of coming out as gay was very important. "I would like to see every gay doctor come out, every gay lawyer, every gay architect come out, stand up and let the world know," Harvey said. "That would do more to end prejudice overnight than anybody would imagine. I urge them to do that, urge them to come out. Only that way will we start to achieve our rights."

Harvey felt that as long as straight people thought they didn't know any gay people, they could believe all kinds of terrible things about them. But if gay people came out, then everyone would realize that there were gay people in their lives—in their workplaces, among their friends, even in their own families. They would realize that their negative beliefs, stereotypes, and misconceptions were untrue.

Harvey didn't focus only on gay rights. When he ran for office, he promised to champion free public transportation, create low-income housing, and support day care centers for working mothers. After he was elected, he succeeded in getting a bill passed that banned discrimination based on sexual orientation—a ground-breaking accomplishment in the late 1970s. He also helped defeat proposed state legislation that would have banned gay teachers, as well as anyone who supported gay rights, from working in California public schools.

In Harvey Milk's lifetime, the LGBTQ+ rights movement was still in its early days. Homophobia was widespread and often led to violence. Harvey knew that by being an activist—and by being a proud, openly gay man—he was taking a risk. He even predicted that he might be killed because of it. Yet he chose to take that risk because he believed in the importance of the work he was doing.

Harvey Milk was only forty-eight years old when he and Mayor George Moscone were shot by Dan White, a city supervisor. His death was tragic, but his legacy lives on. Today, there are more than five hundred openly LGBTQ+ elected officials in the United States. And though there is still much work to be done, the LGBTQ+ community has made great strides since his death. In North America, as well as in many countries around the world, LGBTQ+ people are more visible, more accepted, and have more legal rights and protections than at any other time in history.

Today, Harvey Milk is one of best-known figures in United States gay history, but many earlier activists helped pave the way before him. Phyllis Lyon and Del Martin were two of them. In 1955, they founded the first organization for lesbians. At that time, it was difficult and dangerous to be openly gay or lesbian—you could lose your job or your housing, and you could even be arrested. The two women named their organization the Daughters of Bilitis, after a fictional lesbian character from a French poem. That way, if anyone asked, the women could say that it was just a poetry club. A few years earlier, a group of gay men had started an organization called the Mattachine Society. These two groups helped lay the groundwork for the LGBTQ+ movement.

Dolores Huerta

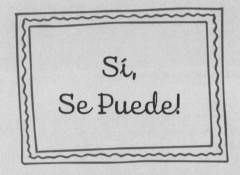

Sí,
Se Puede!

You've probably heard the Spanish phrase *"Sí, se puede."* Barack Obama adopted the English version, "Yes, we can," as his presidential campaign slogan. But you might not know that its roots are in the struggles of working-class Latinos—or that, in the 1970s, it was the rallying cry of the United Farm Workers of America labor union. It was first used by Dolores Huerta, who fought for fair working conditions and the rights of workers, women, and immigrants.

Dolores Fernandez was born in 1930 in Dawson, New Mexico, a small mining community that is now a ghost town, with just a few buildings and the cemetery still standing. She was the second of three children of Juan Fernandez, a coal miner who was the son of Mexican immigrants, and Alicia Chavez, a third-generation New Mexican.

People who knew Dolores when she was young describe her as a bright and active girl. Even when she was small, she had a lot to say! Her grandfather Herculano Chavez called her Seven Tongues because she was such a chatterbox.

Dolores loved her grandfather very much. After her parents split up, when she was three years old, her mother took the children to Stockton, California.

Herculano looked after Dolores and her brothers while their mom worked. As a child, Dolores liked listening to corridos—Mexican ballads that often tell stories about oppression and history. She had no idea that someday many corridos would be written about her.

Dolores rarely saw her father after her parents separated, but he had an important influence on her life. He stayed in New Mexico and became a labor organizer, and later he served in the state legislature. His example may have inspired Dolores to become interested in the labor movement and politics later in life.

Dolores's mother worked hard to support her family. She had multiple jobs, working in a cannery at night and as a waitress by day. Dolores later described her mother as quiet, but "very effective at whatever she did, and very ambitious."

Eventually, Alicia Chavez saved enough money to open a restaurant and later remarried. When World War II broke out, she gave up the restaurant and bought a hotel. "All the family lived there," Dolores explained. "It was a 70-room hotel, a real big one. We kids had to do all the work. We were janitors; we had to do the laundry and iron the towels, iron the sheets, and take care of business, and so she was able to provide for us."

Dolores enjoyed the liveliness of their community in California, with its rich cultural diversity: there were Chinese restaurants, Mexican pool halls, Filipino bakeries. "There were Chinese, Latinos, Native Americans, Blacks, Japanese, Italians, and others," she said. "We were all rather poor, but it was an integrated community."

That changed when Dolores started high school. Her elementary school had been diverse, but high school was divided into cliques according to economic status, and racial discrimination was a constant problem. There were the rich kids, and then there were the poor kids, like Dolores and her brothers. "My four years in high school hit me very hard and it took me a long time to get over it," she later said.

One experience was particularly devastating. Dolores was an excellent student, and she had been earning straight As on her writing all year long, but at the end of the year, her teacher said that she couldn't give Dolores an A. She claimed that the papers were too well written, and she accused Dolores of having someone else write them for her. "That really discouraged me because I used to stay up all night and think, and try to make every paper different, and try to put words in there that I thought were nice. Well, it just kind of crushed me," Dolores said.

During her teens, Dolores grew increasingly aware of the injustices around her. She witnessed police brutality against Mexican and black people, including kids she had grown up with. Even her own family was affected. Her brother was once beaten by a group of white men just because he was wearing a zoot suit, a popular fashion at the time.

Dolores cared deeply about her community, and she was troubled by what she saw. "You find out that justice is not there, the equality isn't there," she said.

When Dolores was seventeen, her mother took her on a trip to Mexico City. It was a powerful experience. The trip, Dolores said, "opened my eyes to the fact that there was nothing wrong with Chicanos. I felt inside that everybody was wrong and I was right. They were wrong in beating up people in the streets and all of the things they did to people." By her late teens, Dolores was developing a strong belief that social change was needed.

One of the most important influences in Dolores's life was her mother. Alicia Chavez was an intelligent and assertive woman, and she helped shape her daughter's attitudes. The family home was egalitarian, and Dolores and her brothers shared household tasks equally. She was never expected to cook for her brothers or do their laundry, as she saw girls doing in more traditional families. "I think my mother was a feminist for her time," Dolores once said.

Dolores's mother was also known for her kindness. She often let migrant workers stay in the hotel for affordable rates; sometimes she even let them stay for free. "They earn so little that they need every penny," she explained to her children.

The farms in California relied on migrant workers. They picked fruit by hand and worked long hours, but were paid very little. Many of the workers would travel to harvest whichever crops were in season—peas and lettuce in winter, cherries and beans in spring, corn and grapes in summer, and cotton in fall. Kids often worked in the fields alongside their parents, and they rarely had access to a good education.

The working conditions and pesticides posed risks to the workers' health, and many workers were abused by their employers. But the owners of the farms were powerful and wealthy, and the workers feared that if they protested the poor treatment or demanded fair pay, they would lose their jobs.

"When we were very small," Dolores recalled later, "my mother would always say to us, 'When you see that somebody needs something, don't wait to be asked. If you see somebody who needs something, you do it.'" So, while she was still in her teens, Dolores joined a group that helped the families of farmworkers. Her mother was active in community organizations and her church, and she always encouraged Dolores to get involved in youth activities: violin lessons, dance lessons, piano lessons, the church choir, girl scouts. Like her mother, Dolores became the kind of person who got things done. It's not surprising that the rallying cry *"Sí, se puede"* came from her.

After high school, Dolores earned a teaching degree and started working in an elementary school. Her students were the children of poor migrant workers, and her experiences with them set her on a path as a community organizer and social justice activist. She became a major force in organizing California's farmworkers; with Cesar Chavez, she co-founded the National Farmworkers Association, which later became the United Farm Workers (UFW).

Dolores Huerta has received numerous awards for her community service and advocacy for the rights of workers, immigrants, and women, including the Presidential Medal of Freedom. She was the first Latina to be recognized in the National Women's Hall of Fame. Now in her late eighties, she continues her fight for a better and more just world.

Dolores Huerta's partner in starting the United Farm Workers was an activist named Cesar Chavez. Before he began organizing farm workers, he had been one himself. Cesar was born in Arizona, but his family was cheated out of the home they lived in, and when he was about eleven years old, they moved to California to become migrant workers. After grade eight, he quit school to work full-time in the fields. He hadn't much liked school anyway. Because his family moved so often, he and his brother attended more than thirty different schools, and many of the teachers forbade them from speaking Spanish, the language that Cesar spoke at home. Although he didn't have good experiences in school as a child, he was passionate about teaching and learning later in his life. He once said that the goal of all education should be service to others. Cesar is one of America's heroes: a labor leader, community organizer, and champion of nonviolent social change.

PART
TWO

TAKING
A
STAND

DISCRIMINATION, POVERTY,

AND OPPRESSION.

WHEN THESE

KID ACTIVISTS

GREW UP, THEY BECAME

HEROES

who transformed
their countries—

BUT THEY LEARNED FIRSTHAND ABOUT

INJUSTICE

WHEN THEY WERE STILL CHILDREN.

Rosa Parks

Taking a Stand by Taking a Seat

Rosa Parks is famous for refusing to give up her seat for a white passenger on a public bus in Montgomery, Alabama. But before her courageous act changed the course of U.S. history, Rosa had to learn to stand up for herself. Fortunately, she was surrounded by family members and teachers who taught her how to be strong in tough situations.

Rosa grew up at a time when racial discrimination was still legal in the southern United States. She was born in 1913 in the tiny town of Tuskegee, Alabama. Her father, James McCauley, was a carpenter, and her mother, Leona, was a school teacher. They had married on April 12, 1912, the same day the *Titanic* set sail for New York City.

Rosa's family didn't stay in Tuskegee for long. The reason they left? Bugs! Specifically, boll weevils: small gray beetles with long snouts that feed on cotton buds and flowers. When Rosa was born, the insects were attacking Alabama's most important crop. Over the next few years, the boll weevils destroyed the cotton plants—and the economy—of the Deep South.

Rosa's parents thought life might be better in the nearby town of Abbeville, so they moved in with Rosa's paternal grandparents. But the house was overcrowded, and Rosa had to share a bedroom with three of her cousins. Rosa's dad was often away working, and her mother didn't get along with her in-laws.

When Rosa was still a toddler, she and her mother made another move, this time to Leona's family's farm in Pine Level, Alabama. Her parents never reunited, and Rosa didn't see her father again.

As a kid, Rosa was shy and often sick. Her earliest memory was of a visit to the doctor. Rosa had chronic tonsillitis, and it wasn't until she was nine years old that her mother managed to save enough money to have Rosa's tonsils taken out.

Her mom was often away teaching, so Rosa was raised partly by her maternal grandparents. She enjoyed being with them, and she especially liked when they took her fishing. She used to bait the hooks for them: "I'd get the worm and he could wiggle all he wanted to," she said. She figured a fish would rather bite a lively worm!

Like Rosa's mother, her grandparents valued education and told her stories from history—the history of her country and of her own family. Rosa learned that her family included people who were black, white, and Native American. One of her great-grandfathers was white. His son—Rosa's grandfather—had fair skin, and people sometimes thought that he was white. He liked to take advantage of their confusion, breaking the unfair rules of the era. He introduced himself by his last name and shook hands with white people. At that time, black men were expected to introduce themselves by their first names, and only white men were called "Mister." Interracial handshaking was also considered unacceptable.

Through his actions, Rosa's grandfather introduced her to the idea that small acts of civil disobedience were an effective way to fight discrimination.

Although her family struggled to earn money, Rosa had fun as a child. She loved playing hide-and-seek and exploring the woods, creeks, and meadows near her home—but she had to watch out for poisonous snakes, like water moccasins and copperheads.

Rosa had a brother, Sylvester, who was two years younger, and he followed her everywhere. "He was always getting into mischief, but I was very protective of him," Rosa said. She was punished more often for not telling on Sylvester for the things he did than for any trouble she got into herself.

Looking back, Rosa wondered if standing up for Sylvester taught her to stand up for herself. "I always had a strong sense of fairness," she said. Once, when a white boy on roller skates tried to bump her off the sidewalk, Rosa shoved him right back. The boy's mother threatened to have Rosa put in jail. But Rosa refused to back down. She said that the boy had pushed her first and she didn't want to be pushed.

Another time, when a white boy named Franklin threatened to hit her, Rosa picked up a brick and dared him to do it. "He thought better of the idea and went away," she recalled.

But to Rosa's shock, her grandmother told her never to do anything like that again. "She scolded me very severely about how I had to learn that white folks were white folks and that you . . . didn't retaliate if they did something to you." Rosa was hurt: she felt like her grandmother was taking the boy's side. When she was older, she understood that her grandmother had been scared for her: "She knew it was dangerous for me to act as if I was just the same as Franklin. . . . In the South in those days black people could get beaten or killed for having that attitude."

Rosa was a deeply religious person. Later in life, her faith became a foundation for her activism. She believed that love could conquer anything, including bigotry, racism, and hate. As a child, she loved listening to the preachers at her church, hearing the music, and memorizing Bible verses.

Rosa also loved school—and books! Her mother taught her to read when she was only three or four years old, and when she started school, at age six, she was thrilled to discover fairy tales and Mother Goose rhymes. She wasn't very good at sports, though. "If I tried to be active, I'd fall down and get hurt," she said.

In the United States at that time, black children and white children had to go to different schools, and the schools for black children weren't as good as the schools for white children. Rosa and her friends had classes for only five months of the year, instead of nine. Sometimes, when they walked to school, the bus going to the white school would drive by and the white children would throw trash at them out of the windows. Rosa and her friends learned to get off the road and walk in the fields when they saw the bus coming.

Beginning in sixth grade, Rosa attended the Montgomery Industrial School for Girls, where she worked to pay her tuition by sweeping floors, cleaning the desks and chalkboards, and taking out the garbage.

This private school for African American girls had been started by two white women: Alice White and H. Margaret Beard. Miss White and her staff had a difficult time in Montgomery: the white community didn't like these women from the north educating black girls. The school was burned down twice. But the two women persisted, and they played an important role for many of their students. Rosa and the other young women learned cooking, sewing, and caring for sick people—but they learned something else, too. "What I learned best at Miss White's school was that I was a person with dignity and self-respect, and that I should not set my sights lower than anybody else just because I was black," Rosa said. It was the same message that Rosa had heard all her life from her grandparents and her mother.

To Rosa, who had grown up in the country, Montgomery was a big city, but it had the same racial discrimination laws as the Deep South's smallest towns. Everything from hotels and restaurants to hospitals and drinking fountains had a sign that said either "White" or "Colored." When Rosa was small, she wondered if "white" water tasted different from "colored" water— and if, perhaps, "colored" water came in different hues.

Public transportation was segregated, too. The bus that went to Tuskegee, where Rosa was born, wouldn't allow black people inside; they had to sit on the roof atop the luggage racks, with the boxes and suitcases.

Black people had been fighting against these discriminatory policies for many years. Back in 1900, they had organized a boycott, refusing to ride the streetcars until the rule was changed. They won that battle, but their victory was short-lived. By the time Rosa went to school in Montgomery in 1924, the streetcars were once again segregated by race. Sometimes when one passed by, she felt frustrated that progress was so slow.

After Rosa finished eighth grade, Miss White's school closed and Rosa went on to Junior High. There was no public high school for black students in Montgomery, so Rosa attended grades ten and eleven as part of a laboratory school at the Alabama State Teacher's College. When she was sixteen, she had to drop out to take care of her elderly grandmother. Then her mother got sick, so she took care of her, too.

When Rosa was in her late teens, she met Raymond Parks, a member of the National Association for the Advancement of Colored People (NAACP). Rosa said he was the first real activist she met. She soon got involved herself, and worked with the NAACP's Youth Council. Rosa encouraged students to challenge Jim Crow laws through small acts—such as trying to take books out from the main library instead of the "colored library." Later, Rosa and Raymond married—and Rosa finished her studies, earning her high school diploma at age twenty-one.

By 1955, Rosa was forty-two years old and working as a seamstress. She was riding the bus home from work one day when the driver ordered her to give up her seat for a white passenger. Rosa refused—the police were called and she was arrested. In response, local black citizens organized the Montgomery Bus Boycott. The African American community overwhelmingly supported the boycott, with thousands of people refusing to ride the city's buses until the U.S. Supreme Court ended the policy of racial segregation thirteen months later. The boycott inspired other protests across the country and brought about more changes to unjust laws.

Rosa Parks never forgot the stories told by her grandparents, the strength of her single mother, or the lessons she learned at Miss White's school. She grew up

believing that she deserved to be treated with respect—
as an equal—even though society told her otherwise. As
one of Rosa's friends once said, no one ever bossed Rosa
around and got away with it. And that turned out to be
a very good thing.

Martin Luther King Jr.

Big Words, Big Changes

Martin Luther King Jr. was the voice of the American civil rights movement. He emerged as a leader during the Montgomery Bus Boycott and helped organize the 1963 March on Washington, where he gave his legendary "I Have a Dream" speech. He fought for racial equality and human rights, and his activism helped bring about the Civil Rights Act of 1964 and the Voting Rights Act of 1965.

As a kid, though, he was just Little Mike: the middle child of three, living in a big house with a large garden, in a middle-class black community in Atlanta, Georgia. Little Mike's father—who liked to be called Daddy King—was a preacher. So was his grandfather. When Little Mike was born, in 1929, both men prayed that the boy would follow in their footsteps.

Little Mike's mother, Mama King, was a school teacher, but she quit her job when she wed; in those days, married women weren't allowed to be teachers. She was also a talented musician, and she insisted that her children take piano lessons. But they were not always enthusiastic about practicing. One time they played a joke on their teacher. Little Mike and his big sister convinced their younger brother to loosen the legs on the piano stool. When their teacher sat down, she went crashing to the floor!

Martin Luther King Jr. remembered his early childhood as being full of love: he later said that life had been wrapped up for him in a Christmas package. He grew up with a feeling of "somebodyness"—a sense that he mattered. But the larger world sent him a very different message.

Little Mike—or M. L., as he was later known—lived in the American South at a time when black people had few rights. White people in power had created laws to keep society segregated, which meant that black people and white people were kept apart. Black people were forced to sit in separate areas on buses and at restaurants. They had to use separate bathrooms and water fountains. They couldn't swim in public pools with

white people or go to school with them. These
segregationist policies were known as Jim Crow laws.

Growing up, M.L.'s best friend was a boy whose
parents owned a store across the street. They played
together every day.

M. L.'s friend was white, and when they started school, they were split up. M. L. was sent to the school for black children, and his friend attended the school for white children. His friend no longer came around very much, and then the boy's mother said that they had to stop playing together.

M. L. was shocked, but his mother was not. She explained the history of black people in America. She told him about slavery and segregation. And she told him that there was nothing natural about racial discrimination. "You are as good as anyone," she said.

Yet despite the racism that surrounded them, M. L and his siblings had many happy times in their childhood. They liked football and baseball. M. L. had a paper route and saved his money. He wanted to be a firefighter when he grew up.

M. L. knew his parents believed in him—and he saw his father push back against inequality. Daddy King had a history of activism, as had his father before him. They had organized voter registration drives and been leaders of the Atlanta branch of the National Association for the Advancement of Colored People (NAACP). Daddy King resisted through smaller, daily acts as well. He used elevators marked "Whites Only" and refused to ride the city's segregated buses. He told his children to avoid supporting segregated businesses.

One day, when a police officer called him "boy," Daddy King interrupted him. *"That* is a boy," he said pointing to M.L. "I am a man."

Another time M. L. and his father went shoe shopping, and the clerk told them to move to the

"Negro section" at the back of the store. Daddy King refused. "We'll either buy shoes sitting here, or we won't buy shoes at all." As they walked away, Daddy King said, "I don't care how long I have to live with this system, I will never accept it." M. L. never accepted it, either. Like his father, he believed that all people were created equal and that segregation violated God's will.

When he was fifteen, M. L. traveled to Georgia to take part in a public speaking contest—and won! But on the bus ride home, the driver insisted that M. L. and his teacher give up their seats for white passengers. M. L. refused. The driver threatened to call the police, but M. L. would not budge. Finally, his teacher persuaded him to stand at the back of the bus for the long ride home. He never forgot the incident.

"It was the angriest I have ever been in my life," he wrote later.

M. L. skipped ninth grade and started high school early, but at first he was not a good student. He was more interested in clothes than he was in studying—some of the other students called him Tweed because of his fancy suits! He liked to dance and play cards, which his father considered sins.

M. L. didn't agree with many of his father's ideas about religion—for example, he did not view the Bible as literal truth like his father did—and after starting college at only fifteen years old, he rebelled. He decided that he would become a lawyer instead of a preacher. That way, he could battle for African Americans' equal rights in the courtroom, like the NAACP attorney Thurgood Marshall.

But at age eighteen, M. L. changed his mind and decided to enter the ministry after all. He realized that he could use his position as a minister to work for racial justice. His father was thrilled! M. L. gave a trial sermon in his father's church—Ebenezer Baptist Church on Sweet Auburn Avenue in Atlanta, the street M. L. had grown up on—and it was a great success.

Soon after, M. L. left Atlanta to attend the Crozer Theological Seminary in Pennsylvania. During his three years there, he studied hard. He practiced his sermons in front of a mirror, developing the skills and style that would later help him touch the hearts and minds of millions of people. He graduated at the top of his class.

M. L. moved to Boston, Massachusetts, where he continued his studies and met a young woman named Coretta Scott. They fell in love and got married in her hometown in Alabama. Life in Boston was good, but they both wanted to fight the segregation in the Southern United States. They felt called to return to Alabama. "We had the feeling that something remarkable was unfolding in the South, and we wanted to be on hand to witness it," he said later.

He was right—but he could not have predicted the significance of their decision. The following year, Rosa Parks's refusal to give up her seat helped spark the Montgomery Bus Boycott, which Martin Luther King Jr. helped to organize. He soon emerged as a central figure in the American civil rights movement. He led protests and organized voter registration drives. He wrote books and articles and gave over two thousand speeches. He emphasized civil disobedience—breaking unjust laws as a way of fighting for change—and was arrested more than twenty times. In 1964, he became the youngest man to be awarded a Nobel Peace Prize. And although he was assassinated at the age of thirty-nine, his powerful words continue to have an impact today.

As a child, Martin Luther King Jr. loved listening to sermons. "That man had some big words, Daddy," he once said. "When I grow up I'm going to get me some big words."

He did. And he used those words to change the world.

One of the people whose words Martin Luther King Jr. studied was Mahatma Gandhi. Gandhi was an Indian activist who used nonviolent civil disobedience to lead his country's independence movement to end British rule. King traveled to India to learn more about Gandhi's work. "Nonviolent resistance," he wrote, "is the most potent weapon available to oppressed people in their struggle for freedom." Gandhi's ideas and actions were an important influence on King and the American civil rights movement, and they have inspired people working for civil rights and freedom around the world.

James Baldwin

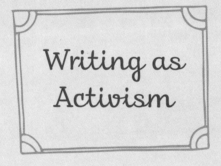

Writing as Activism

James Baldwin was a brilliant writer of essays, novels, and plays. He was also one of the most powerful voices of the civil rights movement in the United States. From an early age, books were central to his life, and he soon discovered that writing could be a way of speaking about—and even changing—the world he lived in.

James was born on a hot and humid day in August 1924, in the Harlem neighborhood of New York City. He was raised by his mother, Berdis, and his stepfather, David. Eventually, the family grew to include nine children.

As the oldest child in a large family, James had a lot of responsibility. He took his younger siblings on errands and to Sunday school, and he helped with baths, changing diapers, and bedtime. "As they were born, I took them over with one hand and held a book with the other," he later wrote.

James's stepfather was a preacher and a laborer, and he supported the family as well as he could. But they were living during the Great Depression, and, like many people at that time, they were struggling financially. For a while, they lived on only corned beef and prunes.

In Harlem during the 1920s, people knew one another and kept an eye out for their neighbors. It was a diverse, multiracial community: African American, Irish, Polish, Finnish, Italian, and Jewish families all lived there. The grocery store owner let the Baldwin family buy food on credit when they couldn't pay. James and his siblings helped out at the pharmacy, mixing and heating giant pots of wax for hair products. They poured it into cans to cool, and when it hardened, they attached labels that said "Dr. Martin's Hair Wax." The candy shop was run by James's aunt, whom the kids called Taunty.

James's grandmother Barbara lived with the family.
She was unwell and rarely left her bed. Barbara had
been enslaved, and her stories about that terrible time
were passed down to her son David, and then to James.

James's stepfather was an angry, troubled man.
He'd led a difficult life, and as he aged, his mental
health worsened. He treated James much more harshly
than he did his younger children. He made fun of
James's appearance, calling him the ugliest child he had
ever seen. James later said that his father frightened him
so much, he "could never again be frightened of
anything else."

However, James knew that his mother loved him.
One of his first memories was of her holding up a piece
of black velvet and saying, "That *is* a good idea." As a
result, for a long time, James thought the word "idea"

meant a piece of black velvet! His mother protected him, and he tried to protect her, too. One time, when he was eight, he stole some money so she could travel to Maryland for her father's funeral.

When James began school, he was very small for his age, perhaps because he was malnourished. One of his teachers noticed and fed him cod-liver oil to help him gain weight. His intelligence was as obvious as his stature, and teachers responded to that as well. Throughout his childhood and teens, a series of mentors helped enrich his education and nurture his intellect.

One such adult was his principal, Mrs. Gertrude E. Ayer—the first black principal in New York City. She remembered him years later as a "very slim, small boy" with a "haunted look." Because of his size and shyness,

James was often bullied. But Mrs. Ayer looked out for him, and she encouraged his talent for writing. Soon James started visiting the nearby public library and devouring books.

James had a favorite hill in Central Park, where he liked to sit and look out over the city, dreaming about the future. The present certainly wasn't easy. As James grew older, the community he lived in became poorer, and local white-owned shops refused to hire black employees. Civil unrest ensued, including protests, boycotts, police brutality, and riots. When James was twelve, he wrote an essay for school about the need for better, safer housing in Harlem.

James's school was underfunded, and each class had up to fifty students. When he was in sixth grade, a young white teacher named Orillia Miller arrived as part of a theater project, and Mrs. Ayer asked her to take James under her wing. Orillia—or Bill, as she was known—became a very important person in James's life. They both loved literature, especially Charles Dickens. Bill and her sister Henrietta took James to plays, movies, and museums. His favorite performance was a production of *Macbeth* performed with an all-black cast. Bill was also an activist, and she included him in many conversations about political issues.

In junior high school, two more important mentors appeared in James's life. Countee Cullen and Herman W. Porter were teachers, and they, too, were black. Mr. Cullen invited James to join the school's literary club and worked with him on writing poetry and fiction. Mr. Porter published James's work in the school magazine and eventually made him editor in chief. As a result,

James earned more respect—and was bullied less—by his peers.

Mr. Porter took James downtown to the public library, helping him see the world of literature as something he had a right to access. His support helped James develop the confidence to overcome the stares and racial slurs of white police officers who would ask why he didn't stay uptown where, they said, he belonged.

The support of Mr. Porter and Mr. Cullen also helped James begin standing up to his stepfather, who wanted James to leave school and get a job. James refused. Instead, on Mr. Cullen's advice, he applied for admission to a prestigious high school and was accepted. He worked on the school's magazine, the *Magpie*. He and the other students involved with the magazine spent many hours in a room in the school tower, talking about politics, literature, history, and religion.

One day, a school friend took James to his church. James soon became an apprentice preacher in the Pentecostal faith and went on to preach in several Harlem churches. This experience taught him a great deal about the power of language and how to use it effectively.

But James's first high school report card was terrible: he failed almost everything! The only subjects he did well in were English and history. He'd spent all his time on the school magazine, instead of studying. He had also been distracted by his struggles with religion: he was becoming more critical of his church and no longer believed what he was saying from the pulpit. He wrote stories for the *Magpie* that reflected his experiences.

James was struggling with something else as well: his attraction to other boys. As he got older, he was beginning to realize that when it came to his religious beliefs, his relationships, and his artistic goals, he needed to accept who he was, rather than run from his true self.

One person who played a vital role in this journey was Beauford Delaney, whom James met through a school friend. Delaney was black, gay, and a preacher's son; he was also a successful painter. He introduced James to jazz and the blues, helping him meet other African Americans who were making their living in the art world.

At sixteen years old, James decided to leave the Pentecostal church and pursue his dreams. His school yearbook photo was captioned with his goal: to become a novelist and playwright.

A ARONOS
hemist

JAMES A. BALDWIN
Novelist - Playwright

JOHN F. BA
Engineer

James was eighteen when his stepfather died. His youngest sister was born the same day. For a while, he lived at home and worked to support his family. But he was unhappy, torn between his artistic dreams and his sense of responsibility. Finally, he decided to leave Harlem. He moved to Greenwich Village and, a few years later, settled in Paris, where he began publishing his writing.

Love was an important theme in much of James's work. His mother, who helped shape his worldview, always reminded her children that people need to be loved just as they are—with all their flaws and weaknesses. When James was a teenager, she told him, "You must treat everyone the way I hope others will treat you when you are away from me, the way you hope others will treat your brothers and sisters when you are far away from them." James always believed that emotional connection had tremendous power to bring about change and improve the world.

In the late 1950s, James Baldwin returned to the United States to support the civil rights movement. He met Martin Luther King Jr. and wrote powerful essays that appeared in major publications. He published novels, poetry, and plays. He also wrote an important nonfiction book about race in America titled *The Fire Next Time*. He joined the Congress of Racial Equality and traveled throughout the South, giving talks on racial inequality. He called for a nationwide campaign of civil disobedience and joined marchers walking from Selma, Alabama, to Montgomery. Through his writing, he reached millions of people—and his fearless, passionate words still resonate today.

Nelson Mandela

When Nelson Mandela was born, his father named him Rolihlahla—a Xhosa word that means "troublemaker." Though occasionally mischievous as a child, Nelson spent his life fighting to end the brutal South African system of white supremacy and racial segregation known as apartheid. After twenty-seven years in jail for his activism, he emerged to become the first democratically elected president of his country.

In 1918, when Nelson was born, South Africa was under British rule. Black people were not allowed to vote, and white people held all the positions of power. Though they were a small minority, white people owned nearly all the land. But as a child, Nelson knew little of this situation. He was born in a tiny village called Mvezo, where, he later said, "life was lived much as it had been for hundreds of years."

Mvezo was home to the Thembu people, part of the Xhosa nation. His father was a chief, and Nelson was a member of the royal household. Like his father, he was raised to counsel the rulers of the tribe and settle disputes. His father was a strict man who had a tuft of white hair above his forehead. Nelson looked up to him. He would even rub ash onto his own hair to make it look like his dad's.

Nelson's father believed that tribal matters should be guided by Thembu custom, not by British laws. So when the British magistrate ordered him to appear, he refused. As a result, his chieftainship was ended and he lost his title—along with his herd, his land, and all the income they entitled him to. Nelson, his mother, Nosekeni Fanny, and his siblings had to move to another village, Qunu. They had little money, but Nelson was happy there.

Only a few hundred people lived in Qunu, which was set in a grassy valley. Nelson's family had three huts, called *rondavels*. His mother made them herself, using mud bricks to form the rounded walls and grass for the roof. The family had fields for crops and a fenced area for their animals, and the food they ate came from what they grew.

Nelson's father had four wives, each of whom lived with their children on their own *kraal*, or homestead. This was a common family structure among the Xhosa people. He traveled between their homes and spent time with his thirteen children. His wives got along well, and Nelson considered them all his mothers. His family's rondavels were always filled with the babies and children of his relatives. In his culture, the children of his aunts and uncles were considered brothers and sisters, rather than cousins. He later wrote that as a child, he was never alone.

Nelson's father was a respected counselor to the kings of Thembuland, and he was deeply knowledgeable about history. This experience made him valuable as an adviser. He was also a wonderful storyteller. From him,

Nelson inherited an interest in the past—in particular, the history of his own people. He shared other traits with his father as well: rebelliousness, stubbornness, and a sense of fairness.

When Nelson was five years old, he began looking after the sheep and cows in the fields. He later wrote, "It was in the fields that I learned how to knock birds out of the sky with a sling shot, to gather wild honey and fruits and edible roots, to drink warm sweet milk from the udder of a cow, to swim in the cold, clear streams, and to catch fish with twine and sharpened bits of wire."

Nelson had more freedom than his sisters, who had to help prepare the food for the family. He and the other boys in the village used tree branches to make sleighs, which the oxen pulled. They slid down hills, using large flat stones as toboggans. Nelson would sled for hours until his backside hurt! He dreamed of becoming a champion stick fighter.

Nelson learned to ride by climbing on top of calves. Once he tried jumping onto a donkey, and it bolted—dumping him right into a thorn bush. The fall hurt, but he mostly injured his pride: his friends were watching, and he was very embarrassed.

When Nelson was seven years old, a man in their community spoke to his mother: "Your son is a clever young fellow," he said. "He should go to school." No one in Nelson's family had gone to school, and few people in the village knew how to read or write. But his parents agreed that he could go, and so Nelson was sent to the one-room schoolhouse on the other side of the hill.

Until then, Nelson had worn a piece of fabric wrapped around one shoulder and secured at the waist, typical for boys in his village. Since he was going to school in the British system, his father took a pair of his own pants and cut them to the right length. A piece of string kept them from falling down. "I have never owned a suit that I was prouder of than my father's cut off pants," Nelson later said.

On the first day of school, the teacher gave them each an English name—and Rolihlahla became Nelson. Like his new name, the education he received was based on British colonial values and ideas.

When Nelson was nine years old, his life changed dramatically. His father died, and soon after, Nelson's mother told him that he would be leaving the village. He didn't ask where he would be going. "In my household," he later wrote, "questions were considered a nuisance." So Nelson packed his few possessions. He didn't know if he would ever return.

He and his mother walked all day long, up and down hills and past other villages, until they finally arrived at the biggest and fanciest home Nelson had ever seen. It was known as the Great Place and was the royal residence of Jongintaba Dalindyebo, the ruler of the Thembu people. Nelson's father had helped Jongintaba achieve his powerful position, and Jongintaba was so grateful that he offered to become Nelson's guardian. Nelson's mother couldn't refuse: she knew that Jongintaba would give her son many opportunities that she could not.

Nelson was sad to say goodbye to his mother, but he quickly became absorbed in his new life. Jongintaba and his wife No-England welcomed him, and their son Justice became his best friend. Nelson took up boxing, long-distance running, and horseback riding. He enjoyed snazzy clothes, and he loved to dance.

Nelson worked hard at school, learning English. And he observed as Jongintaba met with the people who came, on horseback and on foot, to discuss their concerns with their ruler. Whether they spoke about droughts, cattle, or new laws, Jongintaba listened intently. Everyone who wanted to speak could do so, without interruption, and the meetings lasted many hours.

At age sixteen, when Nelson was formally initiated into manhood through a traditional Xhosa ceremony, he was given the name Dalibhunga, which means "creator of the council" or "convenor of the dialogue." Later in life, after he went to university, Nelson became a lawyer. He joined the African National Congress (ANC) and co-founded its Youth League, becoming a leader in the movement to end the system of apartheid. He always tried to follow the principles he had learned in the Great Place: to give all voices a chance to be heard. Even as the country's president much later in life, Nelson remembered Jongintaba's advice that a leader should be like a shepherd: "If one or two animals stray, you go out and draw them back to the flock," he said.

Nelson Mandela had many names during his life. In South Africa, he is often referred to as Madiba. This is his clan name, and the name of one of his ancestors, a Thembu chief. He is also sometimes called Tata, or Father: the Father of the Nation. In addition to his leadership, he was known for his kindness, his sense of humor, his colorful shirts, and his signature dance moves. When Nelson Mandela died in 2013, at age ninety-five, U.S. president Barack Obama spoke at his memorial service:

> "There is a word in South Africa—*Ubuntu*—a word that captures Mandela's greatest gift: his recognition that we are all bound together in ways that are invisible to the eye; that there is a oneness to humanity; that we achieve ourselves by sharing ourselves with others, and caring for those around us. . . . He not only embodied *Ubuntu*, he taught millions to find that truth within themselves."

Nelson Mandela may be known as the father of his nation, but a courageous woman named Albertina Sisulu is thought of by many as South Africa's mother. Albertina—or Mama Sisulu—was an anti-apartheid activist. She was arrested and jailed many times, and for much of her life she was forbidden to leave the area she lived in or attend meetings. Her husband Walter was also an activist and spent over twenty-five years in jail. Although Albertina was closely watched, she managed to sneak political information into her letters to Walter and other activists by using a secret code—she pretended she was talking about gardening! Albertina spent many decades fighting for change and was particularly concerned about the needs of women, children, and the elderly. After apartheid ended and South Africa held its first democratic elections, she kept on working to improve the lives of people in her country as a member of parliament.

PART

THREE

UNUSUAL CHILDHOODS, POWERFUL VOICES

FROM HOGWARTS

TO **HAWAII**

CARIBBEAN

ISLANDS,

VERY DIFFERENT CIRCUMSTANCES,

but each of them went on to touch

THE LIVES OF MILLIONS

OF

Emma Watson

From Hogwarts to the United Nations

Emma Watson was a multi-millionaire by her mid-teens and decided to use her position and her privilege to work for social change. As a child, she became famous for playing Hermione Granger in the Harry Potter movies. But as an adult, she has played an important role off-screen: as an activist for women's rights.

Emma was born in Paris, France, in 1990. Both of her parents were lawyers. She is the older of their two children—her brother, Alex, is three years younger. When Emma was five, her parents divorced and her family moved to England. She lived with her mother and brother in Oxford, but spent weekends visiting her father in London.

Even as a little kid, Emma wanted to be an actress, but she couldn't quite say that word, so she said that she wanted to be a "mattress"! She loved performing, and she was very good at it. When she was seven years old, she won a prize for reciting a poem in a competition.

Emma went to a private school called the Dragon School—a fitting name for a future Hogwarts student.

She liked debating and making art, playing field hockey, and acting in school plays. She also took singing, acting, and dance lessons at the Stagecoach Theatre Arts School.

When Emma was nine, casting agents were looking for child actors for the first Harry Potter movie. They visited many schools in England. Emma's theater teachers recommended her to the casting agents, and she was asked to audition.

The first audition took place in the gym of Emma's school. With about sixteen kids auditioning, Emma said it felt exactly like a drama lesson. Still, it was pretty exciting. Emma was, in her words, "a major Harry Potter fan"—she was in the middle of reading the third book, and Hermione Granger was her favorite character.

Emma had to go to eight auditions over a period of about three months. When the director called her into his office to tell her that she got the part, she was stunned. She didn't yet know it, but the author of the Harry Potter series, J. K. Rowling, had wanted Emma to play the role from the very first time she spoke with her.

Emma was ten years old when the filming began for *Harry Potter and the Philosopher's Stone.* It was her first professional acting job. She particularly enjoyed acting in a scene where she battled a troll, because she got to do stunts. Emma worked hard, but she had a mischievous streak, too. Once, she and Rupert Grint, who played Ron Weasley, printed out a bunch of stickers that said things like "Kick me." Then they stuck them on the back of Daniel Radcliffe, who played Harry Potter, without him noticing.

When the movie came out, Emma saw it at the same time as her friends and she was relieved that they liked it. "It's really weird seeing myself really big!" she commented. She was already looking ahead to the second movie, in which her character would get to turn into a cat. Emma loved cats and had two as pets.

That first Harry Potter movie ended up leading to seven more. Because Emma was so busy acting for the next ten years, most of her education took place on movie sets. She and the other child actors were tutored for three to five hours each day (but had no homework!).

Emma was like the character of Hermione in some ways: she was clever, she studied hard, and she really wanted to do a good job. She didn't just learn her own lines, she learned everyone else's, too. Sometimes, during filming, she would accidentally mouth the words of another character while still on camera. To Emma's embarrassment, they would have to reshoot the scene.

As Emma got older, education and learning became increasingly important to her. She took high-school equivalency exams, and she wanted to go to college, but that was hard to do while acting full-time. She was hesitant about signing on for the last Harry Potter film, but she didn't want to let go of the role of Hermione Granger. So, with the help of the filmmakers, she was able to attend Oxford University in her hometown during filming. Later, when she was nineteen, Emma took time away from acting to go to college in the United States.

After the Harry Potter films, Emma continued her education and acted in other movies. She was also taking her first steps into activism. She became interested in fair trade, and she was concerned about poverty and the rights of women around the world. When Emma was nineteen, she joined People Tree, a fair-trade clothing company, and traveled to Bangladesh to visit its partner company.

She also visited the homes of factory workers who made clothes for multinational companies and saw the poverty they lived in. The workers had few rights and worked long hours. By contrast, those who worked for the fair-trade company were paid a decent wage. The trip strengthened Emma's commitment to fair trade and ethical, sustainable fashion.

Three years later, Emma became an ambassador for the Campaign for Female Education. Camfed fights inequality by supporting girls in several African countries, so they can attend school and become leaders.

In 2014, Emma was appointed a UN Women Goodwill Ambassador. UN Women is part of the United Nations and focuses on women's rights and gender equality. She launched the UN's "He for She" campaign at UN headquarters. In her speech, she called for men and boys to join the fight to end gender inequality. She said that she had been questioning gender-based assumptions for a long time—ever since she was an eight-year-old girl who was called bossy! As she got older, she noticed more and more ways that boys and girls were treated differently, and she could see that it wasn't good for anyone.

She decided she was a feminist because of her belief that all people deserve equality and the freedom to be their whole selves.

Emma didn't know if people would listen, but she knew she had an opportunity to make a difference. "You might be thinking, 'Who is this Harry Potter girl, and what is she doing speaking at the UN?'" she said in her speech. "I've been asking myself the same thing. All I know is that I care about this problem, and I want to make it better." She got a standing ovation, and her speech went viral online and was watched by millions.

She may not have a magic wand in real life, but Emma Watson is still fighting for what she believes is right.

From actors like Danny Glover and Angelina Jolie to singers like Nina Simone and Stevie Wonder, many entertainers have chosen to use their position in the public eye to work for social justice. Some athletes have as well, such as the American football quarterback Colin Kaepernick. In 2016, he chose to kneel during the national anthem to protest racial injustice and police brutality against black people. Over the next few years, many other athletes joined him. The act of "taking a knee" has a long history, but Colin Kaepernick's protest helped it become a widely recognized symbol and brought attention to the issue of racism in the United States.

Janet Mock

Speaking Her Truth

Janet Mock is an American writer, director, and producer. She is also a powerful activist for transgender rights. One of the ways in which she has worked to raise awareness is by telling her own story.

Janet's story began in Honolulu, Hawaii. She was born in 1983 into a big—and complicated!—family. She was the first child her parents had together, but her mother already had two daughters, and her father had three other kids. While Janet was a toddler, her brother Chad was born. Not long after, her parents split up. Chad went to live with their dad, and Janet stayed with their mom. She then moved in with her mom's mother, whom she called Grandma Pearl. A strong, outspoken woman, Grandma Pearl rarely left the house without wearing bright red lipstick. She spoke harshly and swore often, but she always made Janet feel at home.

When Janet was born, everyone assumed she was a boy because she had the type of body that most people think a boy will have. She was wrapped up in a blue blanket and given a boy's name. In school, when the students were told to stand in two lines—boys and girls—Janet did what was expected and lined up with boys. But on the inside, she was already realizing that she was in fact a girl.

The majority of people are cisgender. For cisgender, or cis, people, the body they have when they are born matches the gender they feel they are. But for people who are transgender, or trans, the body they are born into does not fit how they feel. That was how it was for Janet, but it would be a long time before she learned these words to help her understand her experience.

In kindergarten, Janet made her first good friend, a girl named Marilyn. She remembers, "Marilyn was the first person with whom I had things in common." Both had brown skin; Janet was Hawaiian and African American, and Marilyn was Hawaiian and Filipino. Both lived with their maternal grandmothers in the same two-story housing complex. And both loved to play hopscotch and tag. They used to run around barefoot together until the bottoms of their feet were black with dirt.

One day, they were lying on the grass in Marilyn's front yard. "Truth or dare?" Marilyn said. "Dare!" Janet replied. Marilyn pointed at a dress hanging on the clothesline and dared Janet to put it on. "That's so easy!" Janet said. So Marilyn dared Janet to wear the dress and run all the way across the park and back.

The dress was enormous, but Janet felt lovely wearing it. She hiked it up and sprinted across the park and back again. At the last minute, one of her sisters spotted her from the balcony and called to Grandma Pearl. Janet ran faster—but not fast enough. Grandma Pearl caught her and smacked her backside.

Janet's sister repeated the story when their mom arrived for her weekend visit. "You're not supposed to wear dresses," Janet's mother told her. She wasn't angry with Janet; she just wanted her to understand the way things were in the world as she had learned it. She thought that Janet was a boy and she wanted her to behave in ways that fit with traditional, rigid ideas about how boys should act.

When Janet was seven years old, her mom had another baby, and Janet was sent to Oakland to join her father and brother Chad. She felt rejected—as if the new baby had replaced her. It would be five years before Janet would see her mother again.

Living with her dad was hard: he always compared Janet to her brother. One time, he decided to teach them to ride bikes by taking them to the top of a steep hill and making them ride down. Chad went first. Then it was Janet's turn. She didn't want to do it at all. "Stop being a sissy!" her father said. Janet was terrified.

"If you don't go down that hill, I swear I'll buzz your hair when we get home," her father said. It was a frightening threat he often used. Janet was very attached to her long curls; she later recalled feeling that a haircut "would cause irreparable damage, cutting the girl right out of me." So she took a deep breath and started down the hill, riding faster and faster. Panicked, she forgot her dad's instructions about the brakes. She was headed toward a busy intersection. At the last minute, she swerved and crashed into a mailbox. Luckily, she wasn't hurt. Her father just picked her up and said she'd nearly given him a heart attack.

That was just one of many times when Janet's father called her a sissy and tried to make her act more like her brother. When looking back as an adult, Janet could see that he wanted her to fit into the world and not be bullied for being different. He loved her, but his words made her feel like there was something wrong with her.

One time, she tried to talk to her brother about how she felt. She said she was different from him and other boys. He said, "I know that already. You don't like boy things."

The next few years in Oakland were hard ones. The family was poor, and Janet's father was using drugs. Gunfire and violence were common in her neighborhood. When Janet was ten, her father loaded her and Chad onto a Greyhound bus for the long trip to Dallas, Texas, where he had grown up and where her paternal grandparents still lived. They left in the middle of the night and Janet didn't even have a chance to say goodbye to anyone. But her grandmother's house was full of family: Janet got to know her aunts and uncles, and she played with her cousins. She loved to spend time in the kitchen, listening to her grandmother and aunts and helping with the cooking. "They were the kind of women I wanted to be," she later recalled.

As Janet got older, she became more sure of who she was. She started telling other kids that she was a girl, and her name was Keisha. "Keisha was more real to me than I was to myself. . . . She was fully me," she later wrote. She knew that if her father found out, she would be beaten, or worse, but being Keisha was worth the risk. Then one day a boy showed up at her house looking for a girl named Keisha—and her secret was out. When her father asked her if she was gay, Janet didn't know what to say. She knew she liked boys, but she hadn't yet learned the word "transgender," so she had no way to explain that she was really a girl. Her father got out the clippers and cut off her hair.

When Janet was twelve, she and her brother moved back to Honolulu to live with their mother. No one in Hawaii knew about her time as Keisha, and Janet saw the move as a fresh start. She decided she would try to be a good son and hoped that if she pretended well enough, her mother wouldn't send her away again. Janet loved to read and spent a lot of time at the library. It was a passion her mother shared, and they bonded over this common interest. Janet's mom loved shopping for clothes, too, and Janet loved to help her.

Janet desperately wanted to be accepted, and for a long time she tried to hide her true self. Then she met Wendi, a confident transgender girl at her school. Even as a young teen, Wendi refused to hide who she was, and her confidence helped encourage Janet to start expressing her femininity. "I could be me because I was not alone," Janet explained. Her family welcomed her new friend, which helped Janet trust that she could also be herself. When Janet began wearing makeup to school, her mother and siblings just kept loving her and letting her know she was accepted. At age thirteen, she told her mom she was gay; it wasn't the right word, but it was all she knew to describe how she felt. Her mom smiled, letting her know it was okay. "I could stop pretending and drop the mask," Janet later wrote.

Janet transitioned during her teens and began living as a woman. It had been a difficult journey, but she felt lucky to have people in her life who loved and supported her. Her experiences left her with a passionate commitment to support and fight for other young transgender people, especially women of color. Janet Mock has been a powerful voice for change and has received many honors for her advocacy work, including the Sylvia Rivera Activist Award.

Many of the people who began the fight for LGBTQ+ rights in North America were transgender women of color. One of the best known is Sylvia Rivera. Sylvia was there the night that riots broke out at the Stonewall Inn in New York City, igniting the LGBTQ+ rights movement. Sylvia was born to Puerto Rican and Venezuelan parents and had been raised by her grandmother. She left home to live on the streets when she was ten years old—partly because she and her grandmother fought about Sylvia wanting to wear makeup. Sylvia was a founding member of the Gay Liberation Front and the Gay Activists Alliance, and alongside her good friend Marsha P. Johnson, she started an activist organization called STAR: Street Transvestite Action Revolutionaries. She spent her life fighting to make the world a better place for the most marginalized people in the LGBTQ+ community—in particular, homeless youth and transgender women of color.

Helen Keller

The Mystery of Language

Helen Keller is best known as an activist for the rights of people with disabilities, but she was also a radical socialist who advocated for many oppressed groups. Before she could become such a strong force for social justice, she needed to acquire language—no easy task for a deaf and blind child at a time when people with disabilities had little access to education.

Helen was born on June 27, 1880, in Tuscumbia, a small town in Alabama. She was a bright and confident toddler, but at only nineteen months old, she became very sick. The doctors thought she would die. Fortunately, Helen survived, but the illness left her unable to see and hear.

Helen spent a lot of time on her mother's lap or holding on to her skirt while she followed her around. She used gestures to make her wishes known, though she knew that other people moved their mouths to communicate. She would sometimes stand between two adults, touching their lips—but when she tried moving her own lips, no one understood her.

When Helen was five, her sister Mildred was born. Helen did not appreciate this new baby at all. Now

Mildred sat on her mother's lap and took up a lot of her mother's time and attention.

As a child, Helen liked to play with a little girl named Martha Washington, who was the daughter of the family's cook. Martha was two or three years older and she understood Helen's signs and gestures. Helen could be very bossy: she knew what she wanted and was prepared to fight to get it, so she usually got her way.

The two girls spent a lot of time in the kitchen. They helped make ice cream, ground coffee beans, kneaded balls of dough, and fed the hens and turkeys that gathered around the kitchen steps. One time, a turkey stole a tomato from Helen's hand and ran off with it. That gave Helen and Martha an idea: the girls took a freshly iced cake from the kitchen, carried it to

the woodpile, and ate the whole thing. Afterward, Helen
was very sick.

Helen had fun with Martha, but she still had no
language to communicate with. She often had angry
outbursts and broke down in tears, frustrated and
exhausted from trying to express herself. When she
was six, her parents took her to Washington, D.C., to
see Alexander Graham Bell—the man who invented the
telephone. He said that Helen could be educated and
told them how to find a teacher.

Helen later described her teacher's arrival as the
most important day of her life. Anne Sullivan was
twenty years old, and she was determined to help Helen
communicate. On their first morning together, Anne
gave Helen a doll. Taking Helen's hand, she used the
manual alphabet to fingerspell D-O-L-L into it.

Curious about this new game, Helen spelled D-O-L-L back to her teacher. She was very pleased with herself and ran downstairs to show her mother her new signs. She was on her way to learning language, but she did not yet understand that this combination of signs meant "doll," or that there was a word to go with every object.

Helen was sometimes annoyed by her new teacher's interference. "She is very quick tempered and willful," Anne wrote in a letter soon after her arrival. But Anne was patient, persistent, and firm. Over and over, she spelled the names of everyday objects into Helen's hand. Helen quickly learned to spell the words back, but she was still just imitating her teacher.

A month after Anne's arrival, they had a breakthrough. Helen was holding her mug under the water spout while Anne pumped water to fill it; as the mug

filled and cold water rushed over Helen's hand, Anne
spelled W-A-T-E-R into Helen's free hand. Helen later
described the moment in her memoir: "Somehow the
mystery of language was revealed to me. I knew then
that W-A-T-E-R meant the wonderful cool something
that was flowing over my hand. That living word
awakened my soul, gave it light, hope, joy, set it free!
There were barriers still, it is true, but barriers that
could in time be swept away!"

Helen needed more than individual words, however.
She needed to be exposed to language in the way most
children are: by being surrounded by it. So her teacher
signed into her hands from morning to night, using full
sentences, new words, unfamiliar expressions. Helen
learned rapidly. She even tried to teach her new signs to
her dog, Belle, by grabbing her paws and moving her toes!

Helen worked so hard that her parents and Anne became worried. She fingerspelled constantly, not even wanting to stop to eat. They took her to a doctor who diagnosed her with "an overactive mind." Anne tried to encourage Helen to slow down, but Helen was unstoppable. She began learning to read and write. She knew that Anne wrote letters in Braille to other blind children, and she began learning to write letters by herself.

One day, baby Mildred managed to grab one of Helen's letters. Helen pulled the soggy paper from her sister's mouth and gave Mildred a smack. Anne swooped in and picked up the crying baby. "Wrong girl did eat letter," Helen told her, fingerspelling the words. "Helen did slap very wrong girl." She said that she had told Mildred "no, no, no many times."

Anne explained that Mildred did not understand Helen's signs, and that she needed to be gentle with the baby. Helen ran upstairs, and when she returned, she had a letter written in Braille. She gave it to Mildred. "Baby not think," she told her. "Helen will give baby pretty letter. Baby can eat all the words." It was the beginning of what eventually became a close relationship between the two sisters.

When Helen was almost eight, she was invited to tour the Perkins Institution for the Blind, in Boston. Helen had been writing to the school's director Michael Anagos, and without her knowledge, he had been publishing her letters. Helen was becoming known throughout the country, but she wasn't yet aware of it. She enjoyed meeting other children at Perkins, and over the next few years, she was an unofficial student at the school. She was given access to a library of Braille books, and it was through this world of literature that she began to develop an awareness of human suffering.

When Helen was eleven, she wrote a story called "The Frost King" and sent it to Mr. Aganos. He was impressed, but it soon became clear that the story was similar to one published several years earlier. Mr. Aganos accused Helen of plagiarism and had her questioned for two hours by a panel of judges. They eventually accepted that she had not intended to copy the story, which had been told to her when she was younger, but Helen was devastated. Soon after, she left the school. Her confidence was badly shaken, and for a while she was scared that her thoughts and words might not be her own. So Anne encouraged her to write about her own life. Helen's article began, "Written wholly without help of any sort by a deaf and blind girl, twelve years old . . ."

During her teens, Helen continued her studies with Anne. She learned to lip-read by placing her hand on the speaker's mouth and throat, and she also learned to speak. She went sailing in the summer and tobogganing in the winter. She loved to ride her horse and walk with her dogs. She met many well-known people, including the writer Mark Twain, who became a great friend and supporter.

It was as a teenager that Helen began developing her ideas about social justice. Anne had grown up in great poverty. She took Helen to visit New York's Lower East Side, a poor area where many new immigrants lived. Helen was deeply moved. She found it hard to understand how wealthy people could bear to live in their "fine houses" while others struggled to survive.

At age twenty, Helen began her university studies at Radcliffe College, becoming the first deaf-blind person to earn a university degree. She joined the Socialist

Party, writing letters and articles supporting the rights of workers and women and taking a stand against child labor. She supported the NAACP (National Association for the Advancement of Colored People), and she fought for the rights of deaf, blind, and disabled people. She became a peace activist as well. Helen visited thirty-five countries, giving lectures and reaching the hearts and minds of countless people around the world. In 1964, at age eighty-four, Helen Keller was awarded the Presidential Medal of Freedom in recognition of her contributions to her country.

In the 1800s, few educational opportunities were available for deaf people in North America. Laurent Clerc, one of the most renowned people in Deaf history, played a leading role in changing that. Born in France, he studied at the National Institution for the Deaf in Paris. After he graduated, he stayed on as a teacher. While at the school, he met Thomas Gallaudet, an American who shared his interest in education for deaf people. In 1816, both men embarked on a fifty-two-day voyage to the United States. During the journey, Clerc taught Gallaudet sign language, and Gallaudet helped Clerc study English. A year later, they founded America's first school for the deaf. Clerc went on to start many other schools and was a great advocate for sign language. In fact, American Sign Language (ASL) evolved in his schools, which is why many signs have French origins.

Alexander Hamilton

An Unlikely Beginning

Without Alexander Hamilton, the United States might be a very different place. He was George Washington's right-hand man, and his courage and strategic thinking helped win the Revolutionary War. He was also one of the Founding Fathers, whose ideas helped create the U.S. Constitution. But he came from the unlikeliest of backgrounds.

Alexander was born in 1755 on Nevis, a steep volcanic island in the British West Indies, edged with sandy beaches and surrounded by the Caribbean Sea. It was a beautiful place but a dangerous one, with earthquakes, tidal waves, and violent storms. Pirates sailed the waters around the island and were sometimes caught and hanged at Gallows Bay.

Nevis was known as one of the "sugar islands" because its wealth came from the sugar trade. Trading ships from all over the world sailed in and out of its port, and thousands of enslaved Africans worked and suffered on its plantations. The number of enslaved people on Nevis was eight times more than the number of white people. Alexander saw slaves being bought and sold on the auction blocks—his own grandfather, a doctor, used to inspect the people who were being sold into slavery.

Alexander's mother owned slaves, and he and his older brother James were masters of a young enslaved boy named Ajax. But Alexander grew up hating the brutality of slavery. It seemed morally wrong that people's lives depended not on their hard work or their abilities, but on the circumstances they were born into. As he grew older, ideas about liberty and freedom became increasingly important to him.

Alexander's childhood was difficult. His parents were not married, which meant that Alexander was illegitimate and remained near the bottom of the island's social hierarchy. He and his brother were called names and forbidden from attending the church school. People were always gossiping about his mother, Rachel.

As a sixteen-year-old, Rachel had been pressured by her mother to marry a much older man she met while visiting relatives on the island of St. Croix. The marriage was unhappy, and after their son Peter was born, Rachel left her husband and child. Furious, her cruel husband had her thrown in jail, hoping this punishment would make her do as he wanted. Instead, when she was released, she ran away to St. Kitts, where she met James Hamilton, the man who would become Alexander's father.

James Hamilton had arrived in the British West Indies from Scotland. He was from a rich family and had grown up in a castle, but as the fourth son he would not inherit this wealth. Instead he hoped to make a fortune in the sugar trade. Unfortunately he wasn't very good at it. Instead of making money, he got into debt and could not afford a ticket back to Scotland. So he took various jobs, met Rachel, and, a few years later, Alexander and his brother were born.

The laws at this time were very unfair to women. When Alexander was four, Rachel's first husband divorced her. He was now free to remarry—but she was not. The divorce papers described her as "shameless, rude and ungodly."

When Alexander was nine, his family moved to St. Croix, where Rachel had been imprisoned. Alexander soon learned about his mother's past; everyone in town knew her history. His parents' relationship fell apart under the strain, and James Hamilton abandoned his family. Alexander never saw his father again.

Rachel was intelligent, resourceful, and hard-working. She rented a house and ran a store on the ground floor. She taught Alexander and hired tutors for him, too. He had more than thirty books—a huge collection for that time—from which he learned history and political philosophy.

Alexander had just turned thirteen when both he and his mother fell ill with a fever. The doctor treated them and Alexander recovered, but Rachel did not. She died beside him, in the family's only bed. That same night, only an hour after her death, officials arrived and locked away all of Rachel's possessions. Her money and everything she owned—even Alexander's books—were given to her first son, Peter. Alexander and his brother James could not inherit because they were illegitimate.

Alexander and James went to live with a cousin, who managed to purchase Alexander's books and return them to him. Sadly, he died soon after. The boys then moved in with their uncle—but in an unbelievable stroke of bad luck, he died as well. Alexander was fourteen years old, his brother James was sixteen, and in less than a year, they had lost their mother, a cousin, and an uncle. They had no home, no possessions, no money, and no one to care for them.

James became apprenticed to a carpenter to learn that trade. Alexander had a good friend named Edward Stevens, whose wealthy family invited Alexander to live with them. Both boys were bright and hard-working; with their red hair and slim builds, they even looked alike. Edward eventually left for medical school in New York, but he and Alexander stayed friends throughout their lives.

By the time he moved in with the Stevens family, Alexander was working as a clerk for a shipping company. He didn't like the job much, but he was very good at it, and it gave him the opportunity to learn about business and trade.

When he was sixteen, the owner went away and left Alexander in charge of the entire company. For five months, Alexander negotiated deals, inspected goods, and collected money owed. He was a remarkably capable young man, and this experience only made him dream bigger.

Alexander wanted to be successful and famous like the men he had read about in his history books. He was fascinated by duels, which were common at the time, and by ideas about death and honor. (Years later he would die in a duel against the American statesman Aaron Burr.) Even as a teen, he desperately wanted to become a hero. "I wish there was a war," he wrote in a letter to Edward, saying that he would willingly risk his life.

But it was his talent with words that would become his ticket to a bigger role in the world. He sent a love poem to the local paper, which published it. A Presbyterian minister named Hugh Knox read it and was impressed. Knox reached out to Alexander and they became friends. Knox made his personal library available to Alexander, so that he could continue his studies.

The next summer, when Alexander was seventeen, the island was struck by a fierce hurricane. The storm uprooted trees and tore homes from their foundations. Boats were thrown onto shore. The seas rose, and huge waves crashed. When the terrifying storm finally ended, the damage was catastrophic. Some people had been killed, and many were injured. Homes and businesses were destroyed. Food and fresh water were in short supply.

Shaken, Alexander sought comfort at the church and listened to Hugh Knox give a powerful sermon. Inspired by his words, he wrote a letter to his father:

The roaring of the sea and wind—fiery meteors flying about in the air . . . the crash of the falling

houses—and the ear-piercing shrieks of the distressed,
were sufficient to strike astonishment into Angels.

When Hugh Knox saw the letter, he urged him to publish it, giving Alexander his first taste of fame. Everyone wanted to know who this talented writer was. When they found out he was an orphan with no formal education, they were fascinated. Hugh Knox took advantage of their curiosity and collected money for his young friend's education. Such talent should not be wasted, he said. Enough funds were raised to send Alexander to the United States for college. In the fall of 1772, he boarded a ship and never looked back.

After he arrived in New York City, Alexander began spending time with people who thought the United States should be independent from Britain. When Paul Revere rode from Boston to New York, bringing news that American colonists had boarded British ships and dumped tea into the harbor, Alexander began writing political texts supporting the protest. He wrote about freedom and slavery, as well as the right to liberty. He was still in his teens, but he was already taking the first steps to becoming a revolutionary leader.

Over the next few years, Alexander Hamilton took the nation by storm, inspiring others with his fiery words. He joined a volunteer militia to fight against the British in the

Revolutionary War, helped ratify the U.S. Constitution, and became the nation's first Secretary of the Treasury. He was committed to building something lasting and just in government, and his legacy lives on today.

Many young people fought on the battlefields of the Revolutionary War. In the 1770s, teens were viewed differently than they are now: if you were not a child, then you were an adult. Both the American and the British armies included teenage boys—and a few girls, too. One such girl soldier was sixteen-year-old Deborah Samson. Pretending to be a boy, Deborah fought against the British for three years. Another sixteen-year-old girl who played an important role was Sybil Ludington. Like Paul Revere, she rode her horse through the night, knocking on doors and alerting the militia to the approach of the British.

PART

FOUR

CHILD
ACTIVISTS

FIGHTING FOR
EDUCATION,
FREEDOM,
** AND **
CLEAN WATER,
THESE
KID ACTIVISTS
MAKE IT CLEAR
THAT YOU'RE
NEVER TOO YOUNG
** TO MAKE A **
BIG DIFFERENCE.

Ruby Bridges

Brave
Little
Ruby

Ruby Bridges is celebrated for something
that should have been completely ordinary:
She was a first grader, and she went to school.
But she was also an African American child
living in the South at a time when black people
were not allowed to attend the same schools
as white people. Ruby was one of the first—and
youngest—students to challenge this injustice.

Ruby was born in Mississippi in 1954. When she was four years old, her parents moved to the city of New Orleans, Louisiana, but Ruby spent summers on her grandparents' farm. As sharecroppers, her grandparents worked hard to grow food to feed their families, and Ruby and her cousins helped. They picked beans and cucumbers, and they cooked and canned the vegetables for the winter. Those were good summers, and Ruby's grandmother always made her feel special.

In New Orleans, Ruby's family rented an apartment in a rooming house. Everyone on her block was black. Many of the families had also come from farms in Mississippi or Louisiana, hoping to make a better living in the city. All the children in Ruby's family shared a bedroom. Eventually, her family had eight kids, so it got pretty crowded. Ruby's favorite part of the house was the kitchen, because she loved her mom's cooking: bacon, eggs, and grits; homemade biscuits; fried catfish; and, best of all, banana pudding and sweet potato pie.

Ruby and the other neighborhood kids had fun together, jumping rope, playing jacks, climbing trees, or playing softball. But Ruby and her siblings had chores, too, and their mom was strict. "When she told us to do something, we were supposed to say, 'Yes, ma'am,' and not too much else about it," Ruby later wrote.

In 1960, when Ruby was about to start first grade, the civil rights movement was demanding equality for African Americans. One important part of that struggle involved challenging policies and laws that required black students to attend different schools than white

students. Six years earlier—the year Ruby was born—
the U.S. Supreme Court had ordered an end to
segregated schools, stating that all children had a right
to attend their local public school. But in the South,
some states ignored the Court's decision. They
continued to allow separate schools for white children
and black children—and the schools for white students
were better funded and had more resources.

In New Orleans, the school board gave an entrance
exam to the black children to see if they could attend a
white school. The test was hard—the officials wanted
the children to fail. But Ruby Bridges and five others
passed. So the summer before Ruby was to start first
grade, members of the NAACP (National Association
for the Advancement of Colored People) came to talk to
her parents. They wanted Ruby to attend a white

school. They said she would get a better education, and that it would help other black children in the future.

Ruby's dad worried that it was too dangerous, and he didn't believe Ruby would ever be treated equally. But Ruby's mother thought it was worth the risk. "Ruby was special," she later recalled. "I wanted her to have a good education so she could get a good job when she grew up."

Ruby's parents agreed to let her attend William Frantz School. Of the six black students who had passed the test, two decided to stay at their old school. Three were sent to a different school—McDonogh No. 19—and became known as the McDonough Three. Ruby was going to attend her new school alone, its only black student.

When September came, Louisiana lawmakers were still fighting against the court decision and passing new

laws against integration. The governor even threatened
to close all the schools in the state; he said he'd rather
go to jail than let black children go to school with white
children. But the federal judge struck down the new
laws and ordered school integration to move ahead.

On the morning of November 14, 1960, Ruby's
mother dressed her in a starched white dress and tied a
white ribbon in her hair. She told Ruby that people might
be waiting for her outside the school. "You don't need to
be afraid," she said. "I'll be with you." Four men in suits
arrived at Ruby's house. They were federal marshals, and
they were there to drive Ruby to school, which was only
five blocks away. The marshals explained that they
would surround Ruby and her mother on their walk
from the car to the school. "Just walk straight ahead, and
don't look back," they instructed.

As they approached the school, Ruby saw lots of people. She thought maybe it was a festival, like Mardi Gras. It was noisy, and as they passed through the crowd she clutched her mother's hand. White people, adults and children alike, shouted, "Two, four, six, eight; we don't want to integrate." When Ruby reached the school steps, she spotted police officers in gold-striped uniforms, black boots, and white helmets. *This must be an important place*, Ruby thought. The police officers and the big crowd made her think that perhaps she was going to college.

Inside the school, Ruby and her mom were taken straight to the principal's office. The marshals guarded the door. White parents rushed into the school and pulled their children out of the classrooms. They didn't want them going to school with a black child. Ruby didn't know what was going on. All day long, she just sat and waited. When three o'clock finally came, she was happy to leave. But outside, the crowd had grown much larger. They'd pushed past the barricade, and they were shouting horrible things. Worst of all, someone was carrying a coffin with a black doll in it. Ruby didn't understand what was happening, but she was frightened.

Back at her home, the police had set up barricades at either end of the street. They only let people who lived there pass, so Ruby could still go outside to play. She taught her friend the chant she had heard: "Two, four, six, eight; we don't want to integrate." They skipped rope to it, not knowing what the words meant. When her dad came home, he'd already heard the news about the school protests. He called her his "brave little Ruby."

And Ruby had to be very brave. The next day, the crowd of angry, hostile white people was waiting. They shouted racist slurs. One woman screamed at Ruby that she was going to poison her. Inside, a young white teacher named Mrs. Henry met Ruby. Week after week, Ruby spent her school days with Mrs. Henry—just the two of them, because none of the white students came to class. Ruby thought it was strange to be the only child in class, but Mrs. Henry was kind, and they had fun learning and playing together.

Ruby wasn't allowed to eat in the cafeteria with the other students. She couldn't go outside to play at recess, so she and Mrs. Henry moved the desks and did jumping jacks. When Ruby had to go to the bathroom, federal marshals escorted her. Most white parents stopped sending their kids to the school.

The few white families who took a stand for integration paid a high price: other white people blocked their path to the school, shouting and threatening to hurt their children. They even attacked their homes, breaking windows and throwing stones and rotten eggs. By December, school attendance had fallen from almost six hundred students to fewer than twenty. Ruby didn't even know there were other children at the school—she never saw them.

Mrs. Henry did her best to help Ruby. She tried to explain integration. She told her that white people in the South were used to living a certain way and they were having trouble changing. She explained that people were sometimes afraid of people they thought were different.

As the months went on, Ruby began to feel lonely. She asked Mrs. Henry when she would see other children, but her teacher didn't know. That winter, Ruby began having nightmares. She had trouble eating, too. "I knew I was just Ruby," she said later. "But I guess I also knew that I was the Ruby who had to do it—go into that school and stay there, no matter what those people said, standing outside."

Finally, a few white children began coming back to school. The principal wouldn't put Ruby into a class with the other first graders, but she agreed to let them come to Ruby's class to visit. One of the kids refused to play with her, saying that his mom had forbidden him to because Ruby was black. "At that moment, it all made sense to me," Ruby said. "I remember feeling a little stunned. It was all about the color of my skin."

Finally, that difficult year came to an end. The next fall, Ruby began second grade in a classroom with twenty other kids. Most were white, but there were a few black students, too. The protesters were gone, and so were the federal marshals. Progress had been made, and in important ways, the world was changing.

Ruby Bridges hadn't chosen to be an activist, and the stress was hard on her whole family. Later, Ruby said she felt that she had lost her childhood that year. But she showed incredible courage in a situation that would have been difficult and frightening even for an adult.

When she was older, she chose to continue working for justice and equality. She wrote a book about her experiences and traveled the country, sharing her story, visiting schools, and talking to children about racism.

Iqbal Masih

Fighting to End Child Slavery

qbal Masih was only ten years old when he became an activist, and he had already spent six years working in a carpet factory. He knew how terrible child labor was—and he was determined to do everything he could to help end it.

Iqbal **was one of** millions of children around the world who are forced to work for low wages and in hazardous conditions. Desperately poor parents often have little choice: if the family is to survive, the children must contribute financially. Many kids work alongside their families, but others are sold to employers for a small loan. This is known as "bonded labor" because the child is forced to work until the loan is repaid. These bonded children make goods such as carpets, jewelry, and clothes, much of which is sold in North America and Europe.

Iqbal was born in 1982, in a town called Muridke, in Punjab, Pakistan. His parents, Saif Masih and Inayat Bibi, were very poor. Soon after Iqbal was born, his father abandoned the family. Iqbal's mother cleaned houses to make money, and his older sisters took care of him.

Iqbal started working when his father needed money to pay for another son's wedding. The banks wouldn't lend money to a poor man, so Saif spoke to the *thekedar* who owned the local carpet factory. He agreed to lend Saif money, on the condition that Iqbal work for him. Iqbal was only four years old. The factory owner took him into a hot, stuffy room that contained twenty large looms—wooden frames with strands of white wool, known as the warp, stretched from top to bottom.

Children squatted on wood benches in front of the looms. Their job was to tie pieces of colored wool around the vertical strands and knot each piece. Then they used a special tool to tighten each row of knots, and sharp blades to clip each knot evenly so the rug would be smooth. A good-quality carpet can contain hundreds of knots per square inch.

For twelve hours a day, six days a week, Iqbal was chained to his loom! When his training finished, he worked in the factory with other boys, but they weren't even allowed to speak to one another.

The work was exhausting and dangerous. One time, Iqbal cut himself with the knife. The *thekedar* yelled at him not to get blood on the carpet and dripped hot oil on the wound to stop the bleeding. When Iqbal screamed, the *thekedar* slapped him and told him to get back to work.

Tiny fibers from the wool floated in the air, and the children breathed them in, damaging their lungs. Hunching over the loom all day led to bowed posture, and their hands and wrists ached from the repetitive work. Iqbal was always hungry: the meal during his lunch break was small, and the cost of the rice and lentils was added to his family's debt.

The children were watched by a guard, known as the *chowkidar*. "If we tried to escape, we were threatened with being thrown in boiling oil," Iqbal said. "If we were slow, we often got lashed on our backs and heads." Other punishments were worse: children were beaten and locked in a dark closet known as the punishment room.

Despite the threats, Iqbal often spoke up when he thought something was unfair. Once, when he refused to stay and work all night, he was hung upside down in the punishment room. He ran away many times, and even went to a police station to report the abuse. The police officer drove Iqbal back to the carpet factory, where he was beaten badly and warned never to try escaping again.

Sometimes Iqbal was fined for his defiance. With every fine, his debt grew. Other members of his family added to his debt by taking more loans. His original debt was six hundred rupees, or about twelve dollars. Over the next few years, it grew by more than twenty-fold. After working for six years, Iqbal earned only forty cents a day, and it seemed unlikely he would ever be free. He had no way of knowing that people in his country were trying to rescue children like him.

Years before Iqbal was born, a Pakistani journalism student named Ehsan Ullah Khan learned about the horrific conditions endured by bonded workers. He started an organization that became the Bonded Labour Liberation Front (BLLF). Khan went to prison twelve

times because of his activism, but he never gave up. He
traveled to Europe to encourage countries to boycott
rugs made in Pakistan. He started schools so that
children who had been freed could get an education. He
fought for legal change. And in 1992, when Iqbal was
ten years old, the government of Pakistan finally passed
a law ending bonded labor and canceling the debts that
kept children enslaved.

Of course, the factory owners didn't want their
workers to learn that they had rights or that their debts
were gone. Iqbal's *thekedar* warned the children to stay
away from the BLLF, but that only made Iqbal more
curious. He snuck out of the factory and went to a
BLLF freedom day celebration. He couldn't believe what
he heard: there were laws to protect children like him,
and his debt was officially canceled!

From the stage, Khan spotted the child listening in the corner and called him up to introduce himself. At ten, Iqbal was the size of a child half his age—emaciated from poor nutrition, back bowed from years spent hunched over the loom, breathing heavily. But Iqbal bravely joined Khan onstage. "My name is Iqbal Masih," he said. His voice trembled, but he went on to share his story.

After the rally, Iqbal didn't return to the factory. A BLLF lawyer helped him get a freedom letter, which stated that he was free according to the law. But Iqbal wanted to help the other young workers. With the support of the BLLF, he went to the factory and handed the *thekedar* his freedom letter. Then he called to the children: "Come with me and be free."

Khan made arrangements for Iqbal to move to the city of Lahore to study at BLLF's Freedom Campus. It was only eighteen miles from Muridke, but it was like a different world. Iqbal played cricket in the park. He went to the theater to watch kung-fu movies. He studied hard, and when he went home to visit, he shared his new knowledge with his little sister. As he learned more about the world, he wanted to play a bigger role. "I want to be like Abraham Lincoln," he said, "and free the slave children of Pakistan."

Iqbal began traveling with BLLF, attending demonstrations and visiting carpet factories. He told enslaved children about the new laws, and thousands of them followed him to freedom. Journalists and human rights activists from around the world visited Iqbal's school. He enjoyed speaking to them, and his words and stories educated and moved people, making them more aware of experiences of bonded children and more determined to take action to protect them.

In 1994, Khan took Iqbal to Sweden, where Iqbal spoke in a school and at a conference. His activism was gaining international attention, and he was invited to the United States to receive a Reebok Human Rights Award. While in Boston, Iqbal visited another school. "I understand you are studying slavery in the United States," he told the students. "I'm here to tell you that it is still alive."

The students were shocked. They asked him many questions and promised to help in his fight to free bonded children. Iqbal's *thekedar* had told him that Americans were the reason children were enslaved, saying that they liked the cheap carpets and wanted bonded labor to continue. Iqbal said he was happy to learn that Americans were not the demons he had imagined.

Iqbal's activism didn't keep him busy all the time; during his visit, he watched cartoons, saw an IMAX movie, and played computer games. He also went out for pizza, which he didn't like at all! The chef made him risotto instead, which he ate happily; it was much more like the rice he was used to.

When he returned home to Pakistan, Iqbal continued his work to eradicate bonded child labor. His efforts led to the closure of many factories and to freedom for thousands of children. The factory owners were angry, and Iqbal received death threats, but he never stopped fighting.

In 1995, during a visit with his family in Muridke, Iqbal was shot while riding a bicycle. He died instantly and was buried the next day, near his family's home. More than eight hundred people attended his funeral, and more than three thousand protestors, most of them children, marched through the streets of Lahore. They demanded that child labor be abolished in honor of his memory.

The government considered the shooting a random act of violence, but many people blamed the carpet factory owners. Iqbal's death made international headlines, and Western countries canceled millions of dollars' worth of carpet orders. Those whose lives Iqbal Masih had touched wanted to ensure that his legacy lived on. Inspired by his activism, children worldwide have stepped forward to join the fight against child labor.

Malala Yousafzai

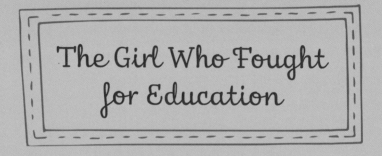

The Girl Who Fought for Education

Fifteen-year-old Malala Yousafzai was on the school bus when a group of men boarded. "Who is Malala?" one of them said. No one spoke, but everyone looked at Malala. The man lifted a gun and shot her in the head. Malala's powerful voice had made her a target for those who wanted to silence her. But this horrific act of violence wasn't the end of Malala's story—and it wasn't the beginning, either.

Malala was born in Pakistan in 1997. Her family is Pashtun: a people of many tribes who live in both Pakistan and Afghanistan. When boys were born in their community, everyone celebrated. The birth of a daughter was usually a much less joyous occasion—but Malala's father was different from most Pashtun men. He asked his friends to throw sweets and coins into her cradle, as they would for a boy, and he added her name to their family tree. Its branches stretched back four generations, but until then, it had shown only the men in the family.

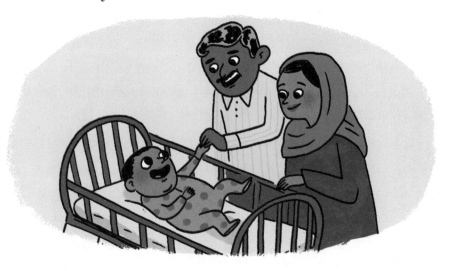

Malala, her two younger brothers, and her parents lived in Mingora, the biggest town in the Swat Valley. Malala's father was an English teacher. He started his own school, where the teachers encouraged independent thinking. "Even before I could talk, I would toddle into classes," Malala later wrote. "You could say I grew up in a school."

Malala was proud to be Pashtun, but as she grew older, she noticed many things that seemed unfair for girls and women. When she pointed them out, her father told her that women had an even more difficult time in neighboring Afghanistan. A group called the Taliban had taken over the country. The Taliban was burning girls' schools and forcing women to cover their faces in public. They had even banned women from laughing. Malala shivered at the thought.

The adults around Malala were constantly talking about politics. But Malala was more concerned about the poverty of children in her own neighborhood: kids who spent their days at the rubbish dump, sorting through garbage looking for things to sell. She thought every child should have the chance to go to school.

When Malala was ten years old, the Taliban arrived in the Swat Valley. The group's leader, Fazlullah, started an illegal radio channel so that he could speak directly to the community. His broadcasts were nicknamed "Radio Mullah." The earthquakes that had recently shaken the valley were a punishment from God, he said, and if people didn't stop listening to music and dancing and watching movies, more terrible things would happen. Malala's father told her that Fazlullah was wrong. "He's just fooling people," he said.

Still, a lot of people believed Fazlullah. Soon, DVDs and CDs were being burned in huge piles on the street.

Malala's family hid their TV in a closet and watched it with the volume low.

But more and more people were listening to Radio Mullah. And every day, new proclamations were made: Men must not shave. Beauty parlors must close. Women should not go to the bazaar to shop.

Radio Mullah also began speaking against education for women. The school was threatened, and there were no more trips for Malala and her classmates—girls were not supposed to be seen outside. Even board games were banned. One day, Malala went to class and found her teacher in tears: the woman's husband, a police officer, had been killed. The Taliban was taking over the police stations.

Finally, the Taliban moved into Pakistan's capital city, Islamabad. The violence escalated, and the Pakistani army sent troops to the Swat Valley to confront them. Fighting broke out in the hills outside Malala's town. School was closed, and Malala stayed home, listening to the gunfire.

Eventually, the Taliban were outnumbered and Fazlullah retreated to the mountains—but the Taliban had not been driven away and Fazlullah still broadcast on the radio. Malala dreamed of becoming an inventor and making an anti-Taliban machine that would sniff out the men hiding in the hills and destroy their guns. Nearly every day, the valley was rocked by bomb blasts.

Despite the turbulence around her, Malala earned the highest marks in her class. She liked performing;

she even wrote a funny skit about government corruption and played the lead character. "With all the bad stuff going on in those days," she wrote later, "we needed small, small reasons to laugh."

Malala's father joined a group of elders to work for peace. He became the group's spokesperson and gave interviews on the radio. He organized a peace march and encouraged his students to speak out against what was happening. Malala began giving interviews, too, talking about the importance of education for girls. But by the end of 2008, the Taliban had destroyed around four hundred schools. And then came an announcement from Fazlullah: as of January 15, 2009, all girls must stop going to school. Malala refused to believe it, but the date was fast approaching.

One day, she overheard her father talking to a friend who worked for BBC Radio. The friend was looking for a schoolgirl who would be willing to write about life under the Taliban. Malala volunteered. Her words were published online every week. It was too dangerous to use her real name, so she wrote under the name Gul Makai. A lot of people read Malala's words.

Then the *New York Times* made a documentary called *Class Dismissed in Swat Valley*. The filmmakers interviewed Malala on her last day of classes. "They cannot stop me," she said defiantly. But when she got home from school, she cried and cried.

The fighting between the Taliban and Pakistan's army continued. When Malala was twelve, she and her family—along with almost two million people—were forced to flee the Swat Valley. Many had to go to refugee camps, but Malala's family went to her mother's village, where they stayed with Malala's uncle. Three months later, the prime minister announced that the Taliban had been driven out of the valley, and Malala and her family returned home.

Her father's school reopened and Malala was happy to see her friends. Best of all, after years of no school trips, she and her classmates were invited to spend a few days in Islamabad, attending workshops to help them recover from the trauma of life under the Taliban. The capital city was very different from the Swat Valley; there, the girls saw that women could be doctors, lawyers, and activists.

Around Malala's thirteenth birthday, terrible
flooding struck the country. When the water finally
receded, her school was filled with foul-smelling mud.
Thousands of people died and millions more were
affected. There was no clean water or electricity. As the
country struggled to recover, it became clear that the
Taliban had never really left. More schools were blown
up, and more people were killed. Malala was scared—
but she was also determined. She vowed to become a
politician and continued to speak out publicly about
education. At age fourteen, she was awarded Pakistan's
first National Peace Prize for her activism.

Malala was becoming well known. Her voice was
being heard by millions, and the Taliban didn't like
what she was saying. Wanting to silence her, they made

death threats. Her father suggested that she go away to boarding school, but Malala did not want to leave.

Still, she checked all the doors and windows every night, and she began taking a bus to and from school, instead of walking. One day, when fifteen-year-old Malala was riding the bus home with her best friend, Moniba, the Taliban found her and shot her. Amazingly, Malala survived the attack. She was rushed to the hospital, where emergency surgery saved her life. The hospital was guarded by soldiers, with snipers keeping watch from the roof; everyone feared another attack on Malala and her family. So Malala was flown to England, where she could get the best care to help her recover from her devastating injuries. When she regained consciousness a week later, she was in a hospital in Birmingham.

Malala's recovery was long and difficult, but millions of people worldwide were cheering her on. After she left the hospital, she and her family stayed in England. With her father, she started the Malala Fund, a charity dedicated to helping all girls receive an education. On her sixteenth birthday, she went to New York City to speak at the United Nations, calling on world leaders to give free education to every child. She received a standing ovation. At age seventeen, she became the youngest person to be awarded the Nobel Peace Prize.

Malala Yousafzai continues to be a courageous and passionate activist for the right to education for girls. She travels to many countries to meet girls who are fighting to go to school under challenging circumstances, facing war and poverty as well as gender-based discrimination. And she makes sure that people around the world hear their stories, too.

Autumn Peltier

Water Protector

Autumn Peltier speaks for the water. She has spoken to world leaders at the United Nations, and she has inspired young people around the world to stand up and fight for environmental rights. Her activism is deeply connected to her Anishinaabe culture. She believes that water is sacred, and that it deserves the same rights that people have.

Safe drinking water is essential for all people—yet many First Nations in Canada still do not have it. Some of these Indigenous communities have been without safe drinking water for decades. Dozens have drinking water advisories: the water that comes out of their taps is murky and must be boiled before it is safe to drink. When Autumn learned about this situation, she had a lot of questions. If the water could make people sick, would it make animals sick, too?

Autumn is from Wikwemikong Unceded Territory, on Manitoulin Island, in Northern Ontario, Canada. She was born in 2004 and began speaking up in her community when she was eight years old. At age ten, she took part in a cultural camp that focused on teaching young people about the land, and through that camp, she was invited to attend the Children's Climate

Conference in Sweden. Kids and teens from more than thirty countries came together to write a list of demands to world leaders, and their message was delivered at the 2015 United Nations Climate Change Conference in Paris. When Autumn got home from that trip, she was invited to the Assembly of First Nations Annual General Assembly, where she gave a speech about the importance of protecting the water. She was already becoming known as a passionate young activist and an inspiring speaker.

In 2016, Autumn released a video in solidarity with the Standing Rock Sioux tribe and their supporters in the United States, who were fighting against the construction of an oil pipeline. The pipeline would cross under the Missouri River, which is the main source of drinking water for the Standing Rock Sioux and the millions of people who live downstream. The protestors were defending their treaty rights and sacred lands and protecting the water, which could be contaminated by the pipeline.

"I am a just a kid, twelve years old. And I shouldn't be worrying about adults' problems," Autumn said in her video. "Kids all over the world have to pay for mistakes we didn't even make. . . . We are the next Elders. We are the next leaders. This is our future. I cry watching videos of Standing Rock. . . . We are only given one planet and we are destroying it. . . . I want us to stand together and we are going to shut down all the highways in North America for a whole hour on December fifth. I am inviting everyone to join us. Bring your shaker, bring your drums, bring your vessels, bring your feathers. Let's pray together." On December 5, Autumn stood on the highway with her mother and others from her community to create awareness for water and to support those protesting at Standing Rock.

Autumn was invited to meet the Canadian prime minister Justin Trudeau. She had been chosen to present a traditional water bundle to him. She spent three days preparing a speech, but she was given only a brief moment to hand Trudeau the gift. Standing in front of him, she began thinking about the government's decision to approve the expansion of the Trans Mountain pipeline. Instead of the words she had planned, she said, "I'm not happy with the decisions you've made for my people."

"I understand that," the prime minister said.

Autumn started to cry. "The pipelines," she said. "I will protect the water," Trudeau told her. She handed him the water bundle: a copper bowl, a red cloth, tobacco, and a small copper cup.

The incident made headlines. "I would like to see Prime Minister Justin Trudeau carry on with the promise he made with me," Autumn said afterward.

The next year, Autumn was nominated for the International Children's Peace Prize. Then came an opportunity that neither she nor her mother had dreamed of: Autumn was invited to speak to world leaders at the United Nations, as part of the launch for the UN's International Decade for Action on Water for Sustainable Development. When the invitation arrived by email, it was so unexpected that Autumn's mother thought it was a scam and almost deleted it!

Autumn and her mother booked a flight from Toronto to New York, but it was canceled—three times! Instead, they drove for fifteen hours to New York City. Wearing a special dress made by her mother's friend from Thunder Bay and standing on a stool behind the podium so that she could reach the microphone, the thirteen-year-old told the audience of international dignitaries that it was time to "warrior up" to protect the water. "Many people don't think water is alive or has a spirit," Autumn said. "My people believe this to be true. . . . Our water deserves to be treated as human with human rights. We need to acknowledge our waters with personhood so we can protect our waters."

Autumn wasn't nervous. She felt that the people there wanted to hear what she had to say, and she used the opportunity to call for international leaders to take a stand. "No one should have to worry if the water is clean or if they will run out of water," she said. "No child should grow up not knowing what clean water is or never know what running water is. We all have a right to this water as we need it—not just rich people, all people." She ended with this heartfelt message: "One day I will be an ancestor, and I want my great-grandchildren to know I tried hard to fight so they can have clean drinking water."

One of the people who inspired Autumn was her great-aunt, Josephine Mandamin. In 2003, Josephine began walking around the five Great Lakes with a group of Anishinaabe women and men, who called themselves Mother Earth Water Walkers. They wanted to raise awareness about how the water was being neglected and to help people understand the importance of protecting it. Josephine walked over 17,000 miles and

inspired many others to walk and take action to protect water. In 2016, she received the Ontario Heritage Award for Excellence in Conservation.

Autumn's mother, Stephanie, has also been an important influence. Stephanie's parents—Autumn's grandparents—are survivors of the residential school system. For many years, generation after generation of Indigenous children in Canada were taken away from their families and communities and forced to attend boarding schools run by the Canadian government.

They spent their childhood years far from their homes, and they were punished if they tried to speak their languages or practice their traditions. Many were abused. When they returned home as young adults, it was hard for them to feel a sense of belonging. Indigenous communities are still healing from the tremendous harm caused by the residential school system.

As a result of her family's history and experiences, Stephanie wanted to raise Autumn and her sisters with a strong sense of their identity and culture. In Anishinaabe tradition, women hold the primary role in looking after water and protecting it. Autumn explains that women are givers of life and that all life needs water: "Women are sacred vessels. They carry the water for nine months while babies are in the womb and so we all come from that sacred water," she says. "We wouldn't be able to live without water. Nothing would."

Autumn is a busy teenager. She hangs out with her friends and family. She enjoys painting and writing in her journal. She loves running and is on a competitive gymnastics team. She attends traditional ceremonies and dances in pow wows. She plays with her dogs: Jaxx, a husky–wolf cross, and Montgomery, an American bulldog. And she deals with regular kid problems, like coping with bullying at school.

But she is deeply committed to protecting water. She has received many awards for her activism, including the WeDay Award for Youth in Action, and the Ontario Junior Citizen Award. She was honored by the Assembly of First Nations as a Water Protector, given the Sovereign's Medal for Volunteers by Ontario's lieutenant governor, and honored as a Water Leader by Ottawa Riverkeeper. She has been nominated twice for the International Children's Peace Prize. Autumn's influential voice and deeply felt words have reached millions, raising awareness about the importance of water and the need to protect it. Because of her, many people have been inspired to step forward, speak up, and take action.

Autumn Peltier says that she will continue being an activist for the rest of her life, and she encourages other young people to join her. "Anybody could do this work," she says. "If we all come together, we can hopefully make a big change."

Mari Copeny is another young person who is passionate about the importance of clean water. In 2016, when she was just eight years old, she and other residents of Flint, Michigan had spent two years dealing with contaminated drinking water. Mari wrote to President Barack Obama, who wrote back to say that he would visit her community and do what he could to help. Her letter, and his reply, made headlines across the United States—but Mari was just getting started. Known as "Little Miss Flint," Mari has continued her fight for clean water, as well as speaking out about other important issues such inequality in education. At age ten, she was a Women's March Youth Ambassador. "There is so much you can do as a kid to really help change your community and the world," Mari says. "Never let anyone tell you that you can't change the world, because you can."

Further Reading

Bibliography

There are many great books about great activists, including autobiographies (books written by the person about himself or herself) and biographies (books about noteworthy people written by someone else). The following is a list of main sources used by the author in researching and writing this book.

PART ONE

Frederick Douglass

Burchard, Peter. *Frederick Douglass: For the Great Family of Man.* New York: Simon and Shuster, 2003.

Dilbeck, D. H. *Frederick Douglass: America's Prophet.* Chapel Hill, NC: University of North Carolina Press, 2018.

McCurdy, Michael. *Escape from Slavery: The Boyhood of Frederick Douglass in His Own Words.* New York: Knopf, 1994.

Susan B. Anthony

Barry, Kathleen. *Susan B. Anthony: A Biography of a Singular Feminist.* New York: Ballantine Books, 1988.

Colman, Penny. *Elizabeth Cady Stanton and Susan B. Anthony: A Friendship That Changed the World.* New York: Henry Holt and Company, 2011.

Harper, Ida Husted. *Life and Work of Susan B. Anthony.* Salem, NH: Ayer, 1983.

Ward, Geoffrey C., and Ken Burns. *Not for Ourselves Alone: The Story of Elizabeth Cady Stanton and Susan B. Anthony.* New York: Knopf, 1999.

Harvey Milk

Faderman, Lillian. *Harvey Milk: His Lives and Death.* New Haven, CT: Yale University Press, 2018.

Shilts, Randy. *The Mayor of Castro Street: The Life and Times of Harvey Milk.* New York: St. Martin's Press, 1982.

Dolores Huerta

Bratt, Peter, writer, producer, and editor. *Dolores.* With cowriter and editor Jessica Congdon, producer Brian Benson, and consulting producer Benjamin Bratt. A Carlos Santana production in association with 5 Stick Films. 2017.

García, Mario T., ed. *A Dolores Huerta Reader.* Albuquerque: University of New Mexico Press, 2008.

Griswold del Castillo, Richard, and Richard A. Garcia. *César Chávez: A Triumph of Spirit.* Norman, OK: University of Oklahoma Press, 1995.

Jensen, Joan M. *With These Hands: Women Working on the Land.* New York: The Feminist Press, 1981.

PART TWO

Rosa Parks

Brinkley, Douglas. *Rosa Parks: A Life.* New York: Penguin, 2000.

Parks, Rosa, with Jim Haskins. *Rosa Parks: My Story.* New York: Puffin Books, 1992.

Theoharis, Jeanne. *The Rebellious Life of Mrs. Rosa Parks.* Boston: Beacon Press, 2013.

Martin Luther King Jr.

Carson, Clayborne, ed. *The Autobiography of Martin Luther King, Jr.* New York: Warner Books, 1998.

Frady, Marshall. *Martin Luther King, Jr: A Life.* New York: Penguin, 2005.

Jakoubek, Robert E., and Heather Lehr Wagner. *Martin Luther King, Jr: Civil Rights Leader.* New York: Infobase Publishing, 2009.

Manheimer, Ann S. *Martin Luther King: Dreaming of Equality.* Minneapolis, MN: Carolrhoda Books, 2005.

Sitkoff, Harvard. *King: Pilgrimage to the Mountaintop.* New York: Hill and Wang, 2008.

James Baldwin

Boyd, Herb. *Baldwin's Harlem: A Biography of James Baldwin.* New York: Simon and Schuster, 2008.

Leeming, David. *James Baldwin: A Biography.* New York: Arcade Publishing, 1994.

Nelson Mandela

Mandela, Nelson. *Long Walk to Freedom: The Autobiography of Nelson Mandela.* New York: Little, Brown and Company, 1994.

Sampson, Anthony. *Mandela: The Authorized Biography.* New York: Knopf, 1999

PART THREE

Emma Watson

Dellaccio, Tanya. *Emma Watson: Actress, Women's Rights Activist, and Goodwill Ambassador.* New York: PowerKids Press, 2018.

Janet Mock

Mock, Janet. *Redefining Realness: My Path to Womanhood, Identity, Love and So Much More.* New York: Atria, 2014.

Helen Keller

Keller, Helen. *The Story of My Life.* Edited by James Berger. New York: Modern Library, 2003.

Lawlor, Laurie. *Helen Keller: Rebellious Spirit.* New York: Holiday House, 2001.

Alexander Hamilton

Brockenbrough, Martha. *Alexander Hamilton: Revolutionary.* New York: Feiwel and Friends, 2017.

Kanefield, Teri. *Alexander Hamilton: The Making of America.* New York: Abrams Books for Young Readers, 2017.

PART FOUR

Ruby Bridges

Bridges, Ruby. *Through My Eyes.* New York: Scholastic, 1999.

Iqbal Masih

Fireman, Paul, Deb Bergeron, Samuel Kofi Woods, and Angel Martinez. *From the Pain Come the Dream: The Recipients of the Reebok Human Rights Award*. New York: Umbrage Editions. 2003.

Kuklin, Susan. *Iqbal Masih and the Crusaders against Child Slavery*. New York: Henry Holt. 1998.

Malala Yousafzai

Yousafzai, Malala, with Christina Lamb. *I Am Malala: The Girl Who Stood Up for Education and Was Shot by the Taliban*. New York: Little, Brown and Company, 2013.

Autumn Peltier

CBC News. "The teen fighting to protect Canada's water—meet Autumn Peltier." The National. March 21, 2018. Video, 7:53. https://www.cbc.ca/player/play/1191799875913.

Kent, Melissa. "Canadian teen tells UN 'warrior up' to protect water." CBC News. March 22, 2018. https://www.cbc.ca/news/canada/autumn-peltier-un-water-activist-united-nations-1.4584871.

Onaman Collective. "For the Water." November 26, 2016. Video, 2:18. https://www.youtube.com/watch?v=yscjdOhVJyU.

Sapurji, Sunaya, Mike Karapita, and Cathy Alex. "Autumn Peltier." Profile in CBC News "I Am Indigenous" series. Design and development by Richard Grasley, Elizabeth Melito, Laura Wright, and CBC News Interactives. https://www.cbc.ca/news2/interactives/i-am-indigenous-2017/peltier.html (accessed May 20, 2019).

Zorde, Izida. "The Powerful Impact of Activism: Autumn Peltier on Walking for Water and Standing Up to Make a Difference for the Environment." *EFTO Voice*. Spring 2018. http://etfovoice.ca/feature/interview-autumn-peltier.

Index

They're Little Kids with Big Dreams . . . and Big Problems!

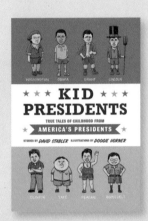